Barbara Walker is a pioneer in faith, in prayer, and in following the Holy Spirit. As I read her remarkable adventures, I became filled with faith.

Dear Barbara, I loved reading your memoir. Your stories and words from the Lord inspired me to greater faith in God and trust that He is leading my own journey....As I read, I was blessed to see how you are using your God-given gifts of faith, leadership, intercession, and teaching. You are an intrepid woman of faith!

—KEVIN MILLER,
ASSOCIATE PASTOR, CHURCH OF THE RESURRECTION,
WHEATON, IL;
FORMER EXECUTIVE VICE PRESIDENT
OF *CHRISTIANITY TODAY*

To me, Barbara is one remarkable, classy lady! I'm honored to be her friend. To say her life has been adventurous is an understatement indeed. Her amazing experiences through sorrows, joys, and challenges, which she shares so candidly herein, reflect her inner strength and are a tribute to her tenacious devotion to God and to all those privileged to be a part of her life.

Barbara's walk with God, as portrayed in the pages of this book, is truly exemplary of what He will do in a life dedicated to Him.

—ESTHER ILNISKY,
ESTHER PRAYER NETWORK INTERNATIONAL

D1234143

Barbara Walker not only lighted the footpath for those who came behind her, but she has preserved it in print for future generations. Some of the paths were in remote places and dangerous situations. As a disciple of Jesus, she wanted her life to be a blessing to others. She succeeded well!

—CHARLES CARRIN,
CHARLES CARRIN MINISTRIES

God Has Been Faithful is an amazing account of how Barbara Walker's life of insecurity and despondency was forever and dramatically changed into a life of impactful healing and restoration. Most notable to me was the Lord's anointing upon Barbara for intercessory prayer, which would take her on ministry assignments to many parts of the world, along with a love for Israel and the Jewish people that continues to this day. Barbara's marriage to Bob Walker, a gentleman and an articulate Christian writer and publisher, brought a polish and serenity to Barbara that beautifully enhanced and deepened her walk with the Lord.

—GAIL NEER, PH.D
CLINICAL PASTORAL COUNSELOR

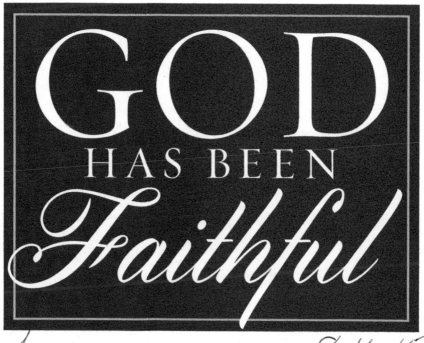

GOD

HAS BEEN

Faithful

To Maureen,   8-16-15
   Thank you for helping me!
May the Lord bless you richly
as we enter the turbulent days ahead.
    Love, Barbara
       John 16:33

BARBARA MELIN WALKER

CREATION
HOUSE

GOD HAS BEEN FAITHFUL by Barbara Walker
Published by Creation House
A Charisma Media Company
600 Rinehart Road
Lake Mary, Florida 32746
www.charismamedia.com

Unless otherwise noted, all Scripture quotations are from The Holy Bible, Modern English Version. Copyright © 2014 by Military Bible Association. Published and distributed by Charisma House.

Design Director: Justin Evans
Cover design by Justin Evans
Front cover photograph: Barbara Walker in Jerusalem

Library of Congress Cataloging-in-Publication Data:
2014953361
International Standard Book Number: 978-1-62998-392-9
E-book International Standard Book Number:
978-1-62998-393-6

While the author has made every effort to provide accurate telephone numbers and Internet addresses at the time of publication, neither the publisher nor the author assumes any responsibility for errors or for changes that occur after publication.

First edition

15 16 17 18 19 — 9 8 7 6 5 4 3 2 1
Printed in the United States of America

To my wonderful children,
Lauri Fox, Eric Kropp, and
Roy Kropp (in memoriam),

And to my five precious
grandchildren, Andrew, Ryan,
Brandon, Heather, and Adam,

And their families.

I am so delighted with the continuing
mission ventures of my family. Several
went to West Africa and to the Dominican
Republic. My only granddaughter and her
husband are planning in October 2015 to
go to Thailand as two-year missionaries.
God's work goes on—and He is faithful!

Contents

Foreword

PERHAPS YOU HAVE just picked up this book and thought, "Hmm, *God Has Been Faithful.* That's a lovely title, but it isn't reality to me." Let my friend Barbara Walker take you by the hand and lead you through her extraordinary trials and challenges, and you will have to say, "Yes, God *has* been faithful!"

Hers is a remarkable journey from spiritual famine to a spiritual faith that will inspire and enlighten you.

Barb will walk you through the minefield of her life, which includes abandonment, rejection, abuse, codependency, addiction, suicide, death, and recovery from a hideously abusive marriage, to name a few. God's healing hand has restored, renewed, and transformed her life into the force she is today for the Lord.

Since surrendering her life to Jesus Christ, Barbara's pursuit of studying, praying, living, and spreading God's Word is truly remarkable. Her Caleb Prayer assignment to Washington, DC, with three fellow prayer warriors was an important jumpstart to her prayer journey anointing. Who would have believed four heroic Christian prayer partners driving a Joshua March around the Beltway in their little silver car could do so much damage to the enemy. Let her pack you in her suitcase and take you on unforgettable travels to Denmark, Sweden, Austria, Switzerland, Holland, Germany, and Russia. She's even smuggled Bibles into China, risking imprisonment or worse. This is one brave lady.

To say she is fearless is an understatement. She knows and practices biblical protection and wields those weapons mightily.

Barbara helps us understand the great truth of God's sovereign control over all of life's circumstances, both good and bad.

And yes, God has been faithful.

She is a heroine of mine. This gracious lady is one of God's choice handmaidens. To me she personifies the Proverbs 31 woman. Strength and dignity are her clothing.

> Charm is deceitful, and beauty is vain [passing].
> But a woman who fears the LORD, she shall be praised.
> —PROVERBS 31:30

P.S. A brief note regarding the marriage of Barbara to Robert Walker. My late husband, Len LeSourd, and I played matchmaker. I mentioned to Bob that I had a lovely single friend. The first time Bob saw her he *knew* she was to be his wife!

—SANDRA LeSOURD YOUNG
AUTHOR, *A WOMAN'S JOURNEY TO FREEDOM*
AND *THE COMPULSIVE WOMAN*

Acknowledgments

Many grateful thanks to:

Lois Easley

Maureen Keil

Dee Lynn

Amanda Quain (editor)

Introduction

I HAVE WRITTEN THIS book largely from a series of journals and with it hope to convey to you, as the reader, a progression of spiritual healing that the Lord has brought me through.

Jesus found me in my brokenness and led me step by step, adventure after adventure, while He was giving me hope and building the way to Him. I found Him who is "the way, the truth, and the life. No one comes to the Father except through [Him]" (John 14:6).

> ...I would like to beg you dear Sir, as well as I can, to have patience with everything unresolved in your heart and to try to love the questions themselves as if they were locked rooms or books written in a very foreign language. Don't search for the answers, which could not be given to you now, because you would not be able to live them. And the point is to live everything. Live the questions now. Perhaps then, someday

far in the future, you will gradually, without even noticing it, live your way into the answer.

—RANIER MARIA RILKE, SWEDISH POET[1]

But seek first the kingdom of God and His righteousness, and all these things shall be given to you.

—MATTHEW 6:33

God does not give us overcoming life: He gives us life as we overcome.

—OSWALD CHAMBERS[2]

1. Ranier Maria Rilke, "Letter Four," *Letters to a Young Poet* (New York, NY: W W Norton & Company, 1993), accessed January 12, 2015, at http://www.carrothers.com/rilke4.htm.
2. Oswald Chambers, "The Discipline of Difficulty," *My Utmost for His Highest*, August 2, 2014, accessed January 12, 2015, at *My Utmost for His Highest: Daily Devotionals by Oswald Chambers*, http://utmost.org/classic/the-discipline-of-difficulty-classic/.

CHAPTER 1

Beauty for Ashes: My Testimony

2009

I was the firstborn of two and grew up in Oak Park, Illinois. I attended the Methodist Church every Sunday with my mother but had a father with a traveling job who wanted to relax on Sunday and attended with us only on Easter and Christmas. His "church" was training for seven years to become worshipful master of his Blue Lodge in Freemasonry.

After confirmation I asked Mom for permission to attend where my friends were, so for high school and college I was a Presbyterian. Then I married a Lutheran. We had three children and ten happy years. He also was a traveling man and died on the road at age thirty-five. I was thirty-three and devastated.

I went back to teaching elementary school, working on graduate hours and raising the children. Five years later I married again and moved with my ten-, twelve-, and fourteen-year-olds to Minnesota. I learned within six months that the marriage was abusive physically and mentally and that he was not interested in my children. I had wanted a father for them.

Within two years I had lost my best friend—my mom—to cancer, twenty days after my firstborn son died in a suicide at age sixteen. At this double loss I was totally broken and turned to Jesus for salvation at age forty. I was the first Christian in my family. I was saved by the side of my bed on October 26, 1972, and received the Shekinah light for one and a half days and *knew* I had been in His presence. I received the baptism of the Holy Spirit a year later on my knees in my kitchen after hearing Father Dennis Bennett speak in the Episcopal church.

I was saved two years into the misogynistic marriage and remained for fourteen more. After discovering his pornography, infidelities, and sexual addiction in 1984, there were three interventions over the following two years with nouthetic counseling with pastors. John admitted his need and agreed to get help but would not, and the separation began. Five years later there was a divorce. My daughter led him in the sinner's prayer before he died a few months later.

I worked for the Lord for seven years, aglow with the awe of salvation. But in 1979 came my Tarsus or wilderness journey for ten to thirteen years. My life was falling apart. I was being stripped to my foundation. I discovered in me a dysfunctional codependent, a bent creature, in whom lies no good thing. I didn't know who I was. I found a compliance that had to be transformed into courage and boldness—and a fear of authority and intimidation that melted as I discovered who I was in Christ and Whose I was. I had to learn to be assertive and to walk in the authority and wield the power of the Lord Jesus Christ where He has given us dominion.

I also had to get into my heart the scriptures we as biblical counselors are so often called upon to use with people in difficult circumstances or without hope. Practically, I am walking this out with small group work; Bible studies here at Windsor Park; with Rez folk (people from my church, Church of the Resurrection) in our home; prayer groups (YPAC—Young Parents of Adult Children); government prayer at Windsor Park; discipling of individuals; and lastly, but part of my call, walking alongside Jewish people.

I believe I am called to edify, to encourage, and to exhort with His truth, to speak a healing word, a discerning word. I believe in passing on to others the exciting adventure of journeying to wholeness in Christ Jesus and demonstrating His life to others by the power of the Holy Spirit.

God has been faithful!

CHAPTER 2

The Caleb Journey

1988

OUR GOVERNMENT PRAYER group had been praying weekly since April 1987. Since January 1988, groups of two or three had been praying for eight weeks specifically for "Washington for Jesus," the nation, and one another. In both of my groups I sensed the urgency to return to Washington, D.C., by car to pray. In the Spirit we had seen boulders and rubble in the path, false motives in some, the party atmosphere of a State Fair, and Jesus, weeping at the sight of the Mall—not high and lifted up over the monuments and the Capitol.

Two women, Dee Lynn and Dorothy Asbury, expressed the same urgency to go—to drive, to pray in unity, to clear those boulders and rubble away, to blow the trumpet, to sound it forth throughout the land that Jesus Christ is Lord. We also sensed a need to wake up the people who sit in apathy and near sleep, to alert the intercessors across the land, to prepare hearts to receive. Another woman joined us, making four little women in a little silver car, our chariot, on a mission. Four from the larger prayer group committed to pray for us daily, as did the two in my eight-week group and our families.

We knew that the angels would go before and surround us. Just as we were heading for the Minnesota border, we saw a sign that read Guardian Angels Catholic Church, and we knew this was the sign that they were with us. We knew that the car was our throne room, and the Lord would speak to us that we were to be wise as serpents and gentle as doves, resting in Him, like yarn in His hand. He would knit us together in unity, instructing us, showing the pattern as we obeyed. We were not to ask why or try to plan ahead. We were to forge ahead in boldness—no fear, using God's mighty weapons against the enemy (2 Cor. 10:4–5). Within a week we left Minnesota, and the first scriptures from the Lord were Numbers 14:8, Habakkuk 1:5, and Joshua 14:9–14.

We checked into our hotel in Crystal City, close to everything in Washington, and the clerk on duty was named Caleb! No one could remember his last name! We knew we had six nights, and if we were to do a Jericho march around the Beltline, we'd better start that night—after driving nine hours, eating, and unloading the car. We chose 10:00–11:00 p.m. to make the 64.4-mile drive around the city and prayed according to Romans 8:26–27. We found ourselves groaning, moaning, and weeping for the sins of our nation and for the apathy of the people. Then we would break into song, adoration, and worship. Soon we found we were sounding as trumpets, sending a clarion call through the night, through the air, in the Spirit, over Washington, to those who had ears to hear.

The Lord spoke to us that first night and said that He would give us "sealed orders" for our mission and that He would open them up before us each day as we prayed.

As day two dawned, the Lord began to open up our sealed orders. The most urgent business was to go into the State Department. Once inside, we didn't get far, except to copy a list of major employees and their office suites. We drove a Jericho march around the State Department seven times during their lunch hour and then parked and walked once around. The touch was important, but we found we could wage in violent warfare in the privacy of our little silver car.

We went on to the Supreme Court, where some of us prayed near the nine chairs. From there we received encouragement from the Council for Inter-American Security and Concerned Women of America offices. From there we found the office building where Lawrence Walsh was heading up special counsel against Lieutenant Colonel Oliver North, and we prayed for the lieutenant as we drove by. We then stopped to pray at the Mall in the car, have supper, then do a Jericho drive around the Supreme Court, bringing down strongholds we had discerned while visiting there. Then we did a second drive around the Beltway, and there was morning and evening of the second day.

Our orders unsealed before us the third day as we searched the Scriptures. One saw a vision of Jesus in His purple robes, and the edges fell over us in a covering, a priestly anointing for intercession for taking upon our hearts the sins of the people. There came on us a deeper anointing of a Caleb spirit, a warring spirit, as we set out first thing in the morning to find the new Russian embassy on Mt. Alto. We had a picture of it and general directions, but everything led to frustration until our miraculous stop by a small park, where Diane approached a man eating an orange and asked him for directions. He came to our car and routed our map. He knew the answer because he had good friends who lived next door to the new Russian embassy and claimed to be furious at the constant interference on their TV from the surveillance equipment. He left immediately for his meeting (a five-minute encounter!) and we found the embassy. Then two of the ladies walked once around this fortress, knowing that large surveillance cameras atop the huge walls were trained on them every second.

From there we found the Panamanian embassy and drove a Jericho march around as well, very grateful for the insignificant little silver chariot as we passed the American security police again and again. Another fierce battle.

From a policeman we got directions to George Bush's home, which we knew to be in the area. We recognized it immediately on the U.S. Naval Observatory grounds near the Russian embassy, which is just up the Potomac from the Pentagon. After praying there we drove down to Pennsylvania Avenue to the White House and Old Executive Office Building and Treasury, all circled for seven times in a mile circle by the ellipse. After fighting traffic most of the day, we thought the salad buffet at the J W Marriott tasted great, and next we did Jericho number three around the Beltline. During this time of intercession, the word came forth of a latter-rain cleansing. Just then, the entire sky lit up as if in response—no thunder, just a flash of light. Once! That was all. We quietly retired, and it quietly rained during the evening and morning of the third day.

It stopped raining about 9:00 a.m. on our fourth day, and we launched out in the sun around 11:00 a.m., thinking we would walk the Mall while D.C. was in church. Wrong! We were traffic-jammed before leaving the Fourteenth Street bridge because of the St. Patrick's Day Parade blocking Constitution and Independence Avenues! So, with plan B in effect, we parked in a two-hour lot and began to walk the Mall. The parade preparations were a perfect cover for our intercessions on the path. Several reminders flashed before us confirming our mission—a little boy threw a rock in our path (to the chagrin of his father). We saw a young man putting on the full armor—literally! We saw and heard the trumpets practicing. There was a Rose of Sharon on one float. We saw a horse and chariot, several swords, and we heard wings rustling in the trees from the wind.

We completed our walk of the Mall within our two-hour time, even walking up the west steps of the Capitol and claiming the territory. Then we drove off to the Hill just before the parade actually began. While they paraded, we drove the two miles around the three Senate, Capitol, and House buildings seven times—reading from Galatians 5 to break power strongholds and loose the fruit of the Spirit. We had brought a picnic lunch and looked forward to eating it in Lafayette Park across the street from the White House. This was not to be, for there was a demonstration of Palestinians getting out of hand there. Plan B took us to a park near the *National Geographic* building where we ate. We crossed the street when we saw another demonstration until we got closer and found it was Jews protesting discrimination in media coverage of Israel. We joined them briefly, then toured the *National Geographic* Museum and bought our special, large-sized maps for prayer. Then we went to the downtown Russian embassy and Planned Parenthood across the street (only four blocks up from the White House). We engaged in more fierce warfare and then a quiet meal in our hotel room before going on Jericho march number four around the Beltline. On our march, Dee had a vision of two angels unfurling a blanket of the Spirit over Washington as a protective shield over the city.

Monday, day number five, dawned cold and blustery,

but we had a day planned on the Hill. We went to three U.S. Senate hearings we had found listed in the *Washington Post*—the IRS penalties reform, Foreign Relations Committee on narcotics, and the Foreign Relations committee with George Schultz on the INF Treaty. Fasting and prayer through all this left us all wrung out, so we revived from the warfare in the Spirit with our evening meal and a Jericho drive around the IRS building. We then drove our Jericho drive number five. As we drove around, I commented that the clouds had broken over the city and were moving out to the east; I could see stars. Just a few moments earlier, Dee, in the back seat of the car, with her eyes closed, was seeing the heavens open and clearing over the city for the angels to descend. Darkness had cleared out. There was blue overhead, so the angels could come back and forth with answers to prayer. Washington was opened to heaven. Praise God! Some scriptures of emphasis included Deuteronomy 7:20–23, and Joshua 24:11–12.

Tuesday, March 15, dawned quickly. This was the day we had waited for, knowing that Nita Scoggan had planned for us to be at a Bible study with her at the White House Old Executive Office Building. This was the day we were to loose the hornets, to drive out the enemy from within the White House. In the Old Executive Office Building we saw a briefing room, the old library, the offices of George Bush and Gary Bauer, and a military conference room being used as a Bible study room, where White House employees seeking strength and help from Him could come on their lunch break in the midst of busy schedules.

After loosing the hornets from the White House, we went back to the Hill to see our senators about the Grove City bill. We met with Christians sprinkled as salt and were encouraged, not by the senators' votes, but by the salt we saw placed strategically, for the senators seemed to have the idea they were elected to use their intellect and not to represent us. It was soon evening and time for Jericho drive number six on the Beltline. We loosed the Lord's plan for Washington, D.C., and the meetings of men and women of prayer. Once again we waged heavy warfare and engaged in the great groaning—howling—for the Lord's will to come forth, to be birthed.

Our final day in Washington was another big one. We met Nita again, this time at the Pentagon. We had Bible study with about twenty-seven women over their lunch hour, then ate in the executive dining room ourselves, where Nita confirmed everything that had happened to us all week. She told us that we were a nation on the verge of disaster. We left with her book, *America, Wake Up*, which she co-authored with her husband, Bill Scoggan, and plans for meeting her again soon. To pray, we took a daylight circle of the Beltline for Jericho number seven. As we left the city, we loosed Michael to be in charge of the angelic host and what happens next. It didn't take long!

We were in a snowstorm in Pennsylvania and pulled off for the night at Jones Mill. We found lodging, then a search for food led us to the White House Pizza House. There on the wall we found a picture of Lincoln's cabinet—with one of them named Caleb—and a historic treasure, an original letter from Abraham Lincoln's pen, written to a mother in Boston who lost five sons in the Civil War. The water stains on it we thought were most likely her tears as she read it over and over again. We ministered to the waitress who had just lost her father. The TV came on with the President saying he had ordered 3,200 troops to Honduras, and Oliver North and others were indicted because of Lawrence Walsh. The hornets had been loosed!

The next morning, very early, Dee saw a vision of an angel in heaven with the sealed orders being stamped, "Mission accomplished!" The final day was all driving—in fact, far into the early hours of the next morning. As we parted with one another, we were asking the Lord if the special guardian angels that had been with us from the very beginning could stay with each one of us. We were tearful as the trip came to an end, for never had we seen the Lord so ever present with us, to guide each step, to pour forth such revelational knowledge and visions, to anoint with such a powerful warring spirit (even though we had never moved in that anointing before), and to bring such unity in our group for every moment of our trip. To God be the highest glory!

And now the boulders had been removed from the road to Washington—the road totally paved. No rocks, boulders, rubble. Our Caleb Journey had ended.

CHAPTER 3

More Adventures in Learning

1987–1993

AFTER THE MIRACULOUS interventions with the Holy Spirit on our Caleb Journey, I sensed a deeper call to intercession. I returned to Washington, D.C., for the rally on the Mall of Washington for Jesus. This initiated many friendships with fellow intercessors.

Over the next seven years, I began regular, frequent trips to Washington, to Virginia Beach, and to Palm Beach County, Florida, where I joined the Esther Network International (ENI), led by Pastors Bill and Esther Ilnisky. This weekly prayer was a continuation of the commitment I had for ten years with our Minnesota government prayer. It led to the International Women in Leadership (IWIL) and Concerned Women for America, to Intercessors for America, and to Breakthrough with Leonard and Sandy LeSourd.

I moved to Delray Beach, Florida, in 1993 to the condo I had inherited from my parents in 1986. During those years, I drove many miles in intercession for America and our leaders. Len and Sandy lived in the same Bar Harbor condo, and he suggested we take a Jericho walk seven times around our condo in intercession. We did, and shortly thereafter the head of management was replaced due to irregular practices.

That led to my speaking about the Caleb Journey at Breakthrough conferences in Virginia and even a chapter in Len's book *Touching the Heart of God: How God Works Through Praying Christians.*[3]

This commitment led to several healing conferences with Frances and Judith MacNutt of Christian Healing Ministries (CHM), which led to a deep friendship with Ann and Frank Lee of Jacksonville, Florida. She is an intercessor with CHM.

I had been regularly attending the Seed of Abraham Messianic Congregation in Minnesota, along with my regular church under Alan Langstaff. When I moved to Florida after Bible college graduation and licensing, I frequented the Messianic congregations in West Palm Beach and Ft. Lauderdale, but mostly attended Ayts Chayim in Boca Raton along with Grace Fellowship's Charles Carrin.

---

3. Leonard LeSourd, *Touching the Heart of God* (Ada, MI: Chosen Books, 1990).

Not all of the friends I met were Messianics. I remember taking the train from Florida to Washington, D.C., with Anita. We stayed at the American Christian House of Prayer for three days, across from the Jewish Embassy, to pray for Israel.

And there was CBN, the Christian Broadcasting Network, in Virginia Beach. I had been in touch with them since I was saved in 1972. I went to many conferences there, even a Feast of Tabernacles event, which led to my involvement with the International Christian Embassy in Jerusalem (ICEJ) and subsequent volunteer work at the Feast in Jerusalem.

God is amazing. All of these connections came because of prayer. While I was working part time at my church in Eden Prairie, Minnesota, and attending Antioch Christian Training School, International (ACTS), I still found time to pray. It was a gift, a blessing, and it turned my heart to thankfulness and joy. I was led out of codependency into a healthy lifestyle of relating to others and adventuring with Christ.

Shortly after the Caleb Journey, I drove my "silver chariot" thirty-four hundred miles in twelve days. I had praise music in the background and was praising God, praying in the Spirit, and claiming the territory, mile by mile, each state for Jesus. I prayed that the people would repent and come to God and that revival would come forth in each heart, in each state, across the land. I learned from Joshua 14:9–14 that Caleb was given the land. I was doing the Spirit work of a Caleb in claiming the land that God had given to the Pilgrims and Puritans that I read about in *The Light and the Glory* by Peter Marshall. It was in the hands of the Anakim in great walled cities, an invisible imprisonment of strongholds and bondages to materialism, greed, lust, and perversion.

> Awake, you who sleep, arise from the dead, and Christ will give you light. See then that you walk carefully, not as fools, but as wise men, making the most of the time because the days are evil.
> —EPHESIANS 5:14–16

CHAPTER 4

My Kairos Testimony

1990

WHEN I BEGAN analyzing the *kairos* times of God's initiative into my life I went back into my journal of remembrance and came upon this passage on my son Roy's birthday, April 19, 1986, fourteen years after his death, from which I quote:

> Lord, bring me into your purpose. What is it for me? In the stillness, seclusion and silence I reflect on the season of time...the season of preparation for overcoming (the Kairos times).
>
> First, reviewing Your care for me in the past fourteen years since my firstborn Roy and my mom died. In my grief I called out to You, and You answered me. I cried out for salvation, and You saved me. You even gave me a thirty-six–hour aura, a touch of heaven so that "I know that I know that I am a new creation and you dwell in me by your Holy Spirit." I asked for a

deeper walk in the fullness of the Holy Spirit, and You gave me what I asked for with the blessing of a heavenly language that the enemy cannot understand.

I asked for help and wholeness, and You not only gave me the years the locusts had eaten from the many illnesses, injuries, surgeries and dental pain of my past years growing up and then having three babies. You brought me through the death of my beloved husband in 1965. You healed a lump in my breast super-naturally in 1974. You healed my bladder and ski-injured knees totally as I struggled to become fit and overcame to receive a desire of my heart to lead a Christian exercise class for five years now! In 1984, just six years ago this month, when I was tempted to run away from the whole abusive second marriage in despair and defeat, You gave me an inner healing at Silver Lake Camp, which helped me to release the lack of love I felt from my dad and to love him the way he is...and You even blessed me with something I didn't even ask for: taking away forty years of allergies! I haven't had one pill or shot or discomfort since!

And with the inner healing I was able to receive the realities of symptoms in my marriage relationship that I was too insecure or fearful to "see" before, the pattern of rejection and hooking behavior to keep me in confusion and self-doubt, the pattern of an addictive lifestyle, even without the alcohol, which led to the second confrontation of two pastors and myself.

You sustained me through six months of tears, even carrying me when I lived alone without the acceptance of my children and my friends. For twelve years You protected me in my own home from abuse and evil, and through my Bible studies and Cursillo community work I kept close to You. Even at work at Colonial, for Young Life, and at Love Lines, You kept me close. I felt it.

And I learned the deeper things through the excellent counselor trainings of Stephen Minister, Lay Counselor Training at Colonial, Contact, CBN Counselor Training through Love Lines, Lutheran Counselor work with Don Richman, Prayer Lines, and now the desire of my heart—Paraclete Counselor Training with Wes Wheatley.

You led me through the grief of separating from my friends and the church that was not feeding me to a church that speaks the Word. I know You are showing me the Way of the Cross, the path of suffering and affliction, the servant leadership that is the Sermon on the Mount to those of us who hunger and thirst after righteousness. If I would follow You I must have the mind of Christ. In order to do that I must let go of the worldly mind, some of my tests being:

- from fear to faith in You

- from resentment to forgiveness

- from angry to patient

- from critical to loving

- from selfish to giving

- from dishonest to truthful

- from pride to humility

- from anxious to serene and calm

- from ungrateful to thankful

- from gossip to holding confidences

- from obsession with self to helping others

- from apathy to purpose

- from false hope and expectation to true hope

- from my failure and weakness to His strength through me

I took a step of faith in 1987 to go through Ministry School at Strawberry Lake, Minnesota, after stepping in faith out of a destructive, fear-filled life of abuse. I took steps of faith to go to China as a Bible courier for six weeks after two trips to Mexico with YWAM. I took a step of faith to say to Pastor Charles Carrin in Florida that I had a vision of a Delray lighthouse before my eyes with its base not on the rock of the sea but on the sidewalk and street of Delray. And furthermore I sensed that my name was Caleb and at my age I was preparing to take the land, though I didn't know why. Charles gave me a vision he had had of the name Jephunneh before his eyes. When he looked it up in Numbers 14, he found Joshua, son of Nun and Caleb, son of Jephunneh, and announced to me that he was to be a Caleb trainer. I fell apart in tears, grateful that I had spoken "silly" words in 1987.

I realized now that these have all been moments of blessed intervention (*kairos* times) that have given security, strength, and direction to my life, to help me to walk by faith and stand, overcoming the storm.

God's vision for my life is now to:

- Be a lighthouse, a safe place for those placed in my care.

- Be a vessel in the hand of God and bring life into others by every step I take, every word I speak, and every place I go, redeeming the land in many nations.

- Assist the Jews home.

- Be in government work and to write.

- Be a prophet and a messenger.

- To give to support the work of the Lord.

- Be an intercessor and to glean like Ruth to feed a multitude.

I went on to missions to Russia, Latvia, and Lithuania; to Sweden, Austria and Holland; and several times to Israel. Then the Lord brought Dr. Walker, a journalist and publisher, into my life, and that's why I'm here at Windsor Park Retirement Community.

CHAPTER 5

A Prophetic Word

1991

I RECEIVED THIS WORD of prophecy in 1991 and felt the close connection to my walk of faith, so I have included it here. It has been proven true over the years that have followed.

Be thankful in all things. Soon this trial will cease. But, there will be a new trial. Each test brings you closer to home, to heaven. As I told My disciples, I must tell you, my little one. As you go from house to house, if you are not received, shake the dust off and leave that house. You will travel as my disciples did in days long ago. Do not fear. It will be a great adventure, because miracles, healings, deliverances will flow. As you see My people you will have deep compassion, for many are broken in spirit and body. Remember now this day what I have told you, my child. Things ahead are not easier, but I go before and behind, and I place My blessings upon your head (Ps. 139). I am your Father, your Husband, and your Deliverer! Hold on! Hold on! Hold on! My ways are not your ways. Keep looking to Me, my child. I know your pain. I know your longing. I know the desires of your heart. I will not give you a stone. I love you, precious one.

CHAPTER 6

Ministerial Training

1992

THE LORD CERTAINLY is in charge, and as I continue to seek Him first He leads me into progression toward healing and wholeness. The Lord laid upon my heart this scripture:

> Blessed is the man whose strength is in You, in whose heart are the paths to Zion. As they pass through the Valley of Baca [weeping], they makes [sic] it a spring; the early rain also covers it with pools [blessing]. They go from strength to strength; every one of them appears in Zion before God.
> —PSALM 84:5–7

I know in my heart that I have stepped from death into life, that I am walking in blessings, that I have crossed the Jordan (even Pastor Alan Langstaff confirmed it in a word on January 19, 1991), and am taking the land, killing the giants of strongholds as I go when they become real before me. Praise God! It was not always so.

I was the first-born in my home in suburban Chicago, Illinois, with a brother four and a half years younger. We were wanted. Mom had a miscarriage between us, but we never knew about it until we were married adults with children of our own. My dad was a salesman and an officer of a men's dress slack company and was on the road weekdays, except for a month from Thanksgiving through Christmas and in the summertime, when business was slow. I know he told Mom that she was not to work or have a car. She was to be in the home with us. She was, and she was my best friend too.

I don't remember much about my childhood except a story about "little miss wait-a-minute," who was always saying that. One day the family went to the zoo, and she wasn't ready and was left behind. I sensed that a spirit of abandonment entered me at that time, and a fear of it too. When I was three I picked up a throat virus that plagued me for four to six weeks every year in the form of fevers, mastoids of the ear, etc., until I had my tonsils out at age twelve. I was in a car accident at sixteen with some internal injuries (I found out years later). I had a serious ski injury to both knees at seventeen, my appendix out at age eighteen in college, and another ski accident at age twenty in Sun Valley.

I married my childhood sweetheart after graduation from Northwestern University in Evanston, Illinois, and one year of teaching second grade. Three children were born to me, and during the second pregnancy I suffered dizziness and pain, and Lauri was born six weeks early.

When she was two months old I had life-threatening surgery to remove two tumors (possibly from the internal bleeding from the car accident) that had grown onto and bent my right ureter, right ovary and tube, and the vena cava. A team of surgeons scraped everything clean in an eight-hour surgery. Three days later the tests came back—benign!

I had to learn to walk again from the extensive surgery, and I suffered from some nightmares from the anesthetic. I went back to the hospital for three to five days every three months for a year to make sure the ureter would not bend and shut off my right kidney again. In all of these visits I was given antibiotics to ward off infection, but the side effects were colitis and the need for gum surgery because the good bacteria left my body with the bad.

My husband, Donnie, was also a salesman but did not have the blessings of December and summer to be around the home, so he would be gone about one-third to one-half of each month. When he was home I would have someone babysit the children, and we would be together with our social friends. Donnie died in an automobile accident coming home from his company board meeting. He didn't own a seatbelt. He was only four miles from home. We had all just gotten over German measles, and he was not feeling well and fell asleep at the wheel. I was devastated, abandoned!

I would reflect here that I had been friends with his

family since I was thirteen. The mother was a chronic alcoholic and the father a foul-mouthed womanizer, a proud businessman who verbally abused us all, and yet we all put up with it. During the first year after Donnie died in May his father tried to hug and kiss me in my home. I found out years later after he had died that he had approached my daughter as well.

I worked towards my master's in education and went back to a full-time teaching job with brilliant third graders whose parents worked at the Argonne Laboratory think tank a few miles away. In 1969 I went to my twentieth high school reunion and re-met John, who lived in Minneapolis. Thinking because of my background of no father on the scene that I needed a father for my children, after a year we were married and moved to Minnesota.

I did some substitute teaching for seven years in Minnesota, but there were no full-time teaching positions open to me. This was a difficult time—a new marriage, a new state, a new house, my children in new schools, no friends—and my kids were entering the teens. John also was a salesman but different from my upbringing. He was selfish, insecure, controlling and given to rage. He was a workaholic and perfectionist and hated himself, but he took it out on me in verbal, physical, and mental abuse.

When we had been in the marriage almost two years I found out that my mom had terminal cancer, and while I was anxious about her, my firstborn son took his own life with a gun at age sixteen. Mom died twenty days later.

Then I was really overwhelmed by grief, having been unable to express the grief over the suicide until she died because of the fragility of her life.

After four months I found Jesus Christ to be my Savior. Both John and I became involved in the Cursillo Movement for the next seven years, and I became works-driven. My usual performance and people-pleasing turned into working for Jesus and the Episcopal Church. Those attitudes were enmeshed in me along with a compliance that I had all my growing years under a rigid authoritarian, distant father, who I perceived didn't love me.

The marriage had been shaky since the first year. I made a vow, which I have since broken, so in codependence I clung to a sick marriage. For twenty years I held on, becoming a very ill codependent, because I didn't believe in or sanction divorce. I grew more and more fearful of his rage, even to losing my ability to speak clear sentences and finish them. He even corrected my English!

It took me fourteen years to discover that John was hiding a sexual addiction. I was desperate for help, and at one point, seeing some friends get help through Alcoholics Anonymous, I went for help for myself with John to be there to "support me" for one month. In group I was confronted and told I was not a dependent. When they turned to John he refused to go back. I still didn't see what was wrong. I knew his father had been an alcoholic, and from what I had learned I knew he was exhibiting the dry-drunk symptoms. Soon after that I began to read M. Scott Peck's book *The People of the Lie* and was shocked to discover that there were some people who were really evil from the inside out. Within six weeks of reading that book, two ministers and I were confronting John with evidence gained from Patrick Carnes's book written a year earlier, now called *Out of the Shadows*. He was gently, lovingly confronted with pornography, and he admitted he needed help. When given a choice of treatment centers and a timeline, he did not follow through, and we were separated.

[I deviate from this journal now to say that in the 1980s issues like sexual addiction were not freely spoken of. (Patrick Carnes's book *Out of the Shadows* wasn't published until 1983.) In Minnesota, no-fault divorce had just been passed and was not a friendly topic in the various church denominations. It was difficult for me to stand up for my rights when I was ignored or the issue was shoved under the rug. I was the first Christian in my family and had to learn how to listen to God, even to the point when He told me to, "Flee!" (like Joseph did in Genesis 39:12). I also had to learn how to rise up with courage and become an overcomer. God helped me, and He is faithful.]

During this separation I took the Love Lines counseling training of the 700 Club. I had been through Contact Hotline phone training and also lay counselor and Stephen minister training, but this was the first

Spirit-filled training I had with hands-on experience. I phone-counseled weekly for three years.

After four months of John's dating me again (romancing me, I thought) we reconciled, and I forgave, but he didn't forgive or change. I began to spiral downward again in codependency over the next fifteen months. We had a major crisis in 1986 when he was upset because I asked him to cut strawberries on a cutting board rather than on the Formica. He came at me, swearing, and was about to throw me through the living room picture window when I cried, "Jesus!" and prayed aloud in the Spirit. He stopped in his tracks. This was all one month after he had been described in a blackmail phone call that I received that asserted that he was soliciting a fourteen-year-old girl!

Finally, enough was enough! In 1986, after the second separation, after my world and my vow fell apart, my fourteen-year-old German Shepherd/coyote dog had to be put to sleep. He was born at the time my son died. Two-months later my dad died, but I had witnessed to him before he died. All those negative events shocked me into reality, and I could acknowledge that I was in a dangerous state of codependence, focusing my life on another and neglecting myself into a self-defeating lifestyle.

Looking back now, I reflect that these were the years that I worked at Antioch, hidden away in a safe environment where I could mend, heal, and grow into the life that God had called me to. I was to be a Caleb, who in his latter years stood courageously and said, "Give me this mountain." Give up these Jews to go home to Israel. Give up this land, Satan—I resist you. Give up, you border guards in China; I'm coming through with Bibles!

I have a support group of two other women outside my church. I have continued taking classes at ACTS. I went through the School of Ministry at Christian Retreat, three Christian healing ministry conferences with Francis and Judith MacNutt, several conferences in Washington, D.C., and a Christian counselors' conference in Atlanta, Georgia. Through all this training and experience I learned about and was healed from dysfunctions in my life. I enclose a short testimony here, which I wrote in 1992:

I realized that I had allowed the enemy, though a human being or several, to convince me that I was mindless, no longer a teacher, of no account, not worth listening to, of no great worth—even unable to finish a sentence. It reminds me of the way my mother was with my dad! I dissolved in tears of gratitude for this truth and soon received inner healing of the hole in my soul, a place where I had been unable to hold on to prophetic words, words of love and affirmation. They drained through me and left me empty again. No more! Like the song "I Will Change Your Name" by D J Butler says, I finally learned that the Holy Spirit wanted to change my identity from a wounded and afraid woman to an overcomer, reconciled with God through Christ!

I have discovered two major weaknesses that I have nurtured through the years of ignorance, denial, and unhealthy conditioning. The first is the abandonment and rejection and a perception of being misunderstood. I did go through a period of reactive depression where I was on antidepressants in 1975, three years after the double deaths. But along with that grief was the constant stress of being in a sick marriage with no accountability and responsibility. The bills were not being paid, even though I was working, and the gas and electric companies were often threatening us. I also, with people-pleasing and performance and manipulating (which I discovered that I had learned from my mom), tried to make it all right for my family by enabling, covering up, and creating more confusion and more stress, even adrenaline highs followed by a crash. (I watch for these now, particularly after a mission trip. I am learning to be good to myself.)

Even now I battle high cholesterol, which is also a reaction to arousal stress and distress. My response to this is to know in my heart that I am not abandoned but the adopted daughter of the Most High. And I learned from my professor that I can call Him "Abba"! Psalm 27:10 tells me as a widow and orphan that, "If my father and my mother forsake me [died], then the LORD will take me in." I did teach aerobics to Christian music for six years from 1981–1987, and I know this was the Lord keeping me in balance for the pain and stress I endured through abuse and then divorce.

My second area overlaps the first, triggered by it, no doubt. It was fear of authority and of male authority figures. I was afraid to speak back to my dad (although when healed, I was, by the power of the Holy Spirit, able to break through his defenses and lead him to the Lord one month before he died at the age of eighty-nine). With the fear of authority I became compliant, a placator, a care-taker, an appeaser, a people-pleaser. I didn't know boundaries. I wanted to do everything, for it was hard to say no and choose. I didn't know I had choices. I gave away my power, my boundaries, my right to choose. Gradually, as the crises grew over the years, I reached the victim's stance of codependence. I was led to a heightened state of anger and hurt and stuffed it, saying, "It doesn't matter." But it does! And gradually I have been learning assertiveness, that enough is enough, and I will walk away from abuse into reality.

The Lord is building courage and boldness into me. In China before one major border crossing I sensed He said to me, "Barbara, it is My power you have within you. Don't give it away. Wield it." I am learning to set limits, to be assertive with firmness and yet with love. I am learning not to be over-responsible but to be dependent on God and to be in control, free of hostilities. I set boundaries as to what I choose to do and not do. I am learning to be flexible and spontaneous and sensitive, having lower expectations. This in turn is building a better self-esteem, how I feel about who and what I am. I am learning that I have rights but also that I can choose to lay them down. I have forgiven, but since the Spiritual Awareness Week, I have understood the cost of forgiveness—that I take the pain when I forgive others. I choose to receive the pain. I am growing, praise God!

I have been set free of fear—irrational fear—and have been tested on the mission field many times since then, and it has not returned. There is still the weakness, the shyness, the holding back, even to being tongue-tied before men in authority. But I am aware of it, praise God.

I have been preparing my personality through the months of team counseling. Many people come with distortions, and my team partner and I are open to the guidance of the Holy Spirit to set the captives free. It is working. One of my big blessings was to go back to Love Lines crisis phones and see how far the Lord has brought me in terms of wisdom in counsel to others. I am humbled and very grateful. I have been setting a firm discipline of reading, homework, of grandchildren, of intercession, of church, of exercise, of having fun—and observing others and nature and taking joy in it all! I am learning to be real!

And I close with the greatest joy I have experienced in many years. It's on Wednesdays, when I take my youngest grandson, who is three, to meet his cousins (ages four, five, and six) and my daughter, and we watch them in seventy-five minutes of Kindermusik, a weekly musical experience. I bought it for them for Christmas and their birthdays, and it goes every week through May. Watching their expressions and wide-eyed participation absolutely delights me! And two of them have already accepted Jesus! Every three weeks I go to the public library to get ten books to read to them. What a joy! I choose life and hope that I am a pleasing light to others. May they choose them too. Amen.

Post Script: Two years after I wrote the above I was flying home to Minnetonka, Minnesota, alone, and a pilot who was traveling but not on duty sat next to me. I had gone through years of diminished self-concept and diminished self-worth and a fear of even conversation with men.

This three-hour trip changed all that. I found that I was able to carry on an interesting and relevant conversation with this pilot that shattered my misbeliefs about myself. Praise the Lord!

Back in Florida four months later I was to meet a giant of a man by the name of Robert Walker. The Lord had prepared me through Bible college, counseling ministry, and missions and was now breaking the strongholds of my mind. We had thirteen wonderful years of ministry as a couple. Praise be to God!

CHAPTER 7

A Project in Faith

1992

I WENT TO ISRAEL in 1980 as a pilgrim, knowing in my heart that I would return to the land someday. I also prayed for everyone I knew by the Sea of Galilee. Four years later I read the book *Exodus II* by Steve Lightle. I was touched in my heart with the call to assist the Jews.

The only thing that was real to me was the call. The circumstances in my life were certainly not enabling me to reach this goal of the call. I was separated and in a deplorable state of codependency, ill from trying to fix the marriage and make things come out right. Circumstances got worse over the next two years. At one point I heard the Lord paraphrase the words to me from Matthew 8:22, saying, "Barbara, you come follow Me. Leave the spiritually dead to bury the dead. You come follow Me." I did, by stepping out in faith, not knowing what would happen. This led to several confrontations of John's addictions, and when there was no fruit of change, a court battle to fight for something from a twenty-year marriage, which was complicated by his denial of the problem after admitting his need for help two years earlier.

During these years I attended Antioch Church, worked as receptionist, and did the weekly bulletin. I also took courses at Antioch Christian Training School (ACTS) International. I continued to seek counsel, and as I began to trust people again, I began to seek the Lord in earnest. Gradually, my shredded heart was becoming strengthened and whole. I began to hear the missions call again. After a ten-week period of sitting at His feet at the School of Ministry at Christian Retreat, I went to Mexico with YWAM to evangelize and give Bibles door to door. I went again to Mexico the next year.

On this Mexican mission trip in 1989, one of the two Mexican bus drivers began to speak of his upcoming mission trip to Alaska to build a place for the Jews as they were released out of Russia over the Bering Strait and flown into Homer. I knew by faith in my heart that the conversation was why I had returned to Mexico.

But this is what was spoken by the prophet...
—ACTS 2:16

With no further leaning to Mexico, the Lord put upon my heart to take Bibles over the Chinese border at a very difficult time, six months after the Tiananmen Square Massacre. When I asked Him if He wanted me to go, the

Lord shouted in my spirit, "Barbara, you *know* I want you to go." I didn't know why. I went, and through that six-week period I learned a lot about courage and boldness, letting go of fear, and of not giving my power away anymore, as I had in the dysfunctional lifestyle. He planted a chip of faith, saying, "Barbara, it is My power you carry within you. Do not give it away. Wield it."

When I returned home it was to more battle in the court. This time the decision of the judge, which had been in my favor, was being appealed, which doubled the attorney's fees. In my brokenness I continued to seek the Lord and His will for me.

I had become an intercessor since 1984 also, going on several Caleb Journeys of spying out the land all over the United States—particularly Washington, D.C. I continued to take classes at ACTS International, now mostly for credit rather than audit. I began to attend meetings of a ministry "to the Jew first" (Rom. 2:10), twice monthly. Here my early words of call were confirmed, and we began to prepare for our first mission trip to Russia.

During the two years since my return from China and the appeal of the judge's decision regarding the state of our divorce proceedings, the legal battle continued. I sold my home, but for much less than the court had appraised it for. I had a garage sale to downsize after forty years of collecting items and moved into a two-bedroom apartment.

I paid for the trip six months after the sale of my home, and then the Russian coup happened. I wondered what the Lord had in mind, because I knew by a chip of faith that, "Thus says the Lord GOD; See, I will lift up My hand to the nations and set up My standard to the peoples; and they shall bring your sons in their arms, and your daughters shall be carried on their shoulders" (Isa. 49:22). In three days the coup was over, and folks clamored for tickets to the new Russia. Upon our return from the two-week trip to Russia we—three women and two male pastors—had the blessing of being asked to be the ambassadors for the northern arm of Exodus II, which had already begun. It all involved faith, not my worry about my money.

As I wondered how I would be able to finance these further trips on such a limited income, the scripture came to me of 2 Chronicles 20:16–17, "Tomorrow go down against them...It will not be necessary for you to fight in this conflict. Take your positions, stand, and observe the deliverance of the LORD for you...Do not fear or be filled with terror. Tomorrow, go out before them, and the LORD will be with you." I had gone to face them. Now I was to stand and see.

I took the step of faith to speak to my lawyer, and he agreed to enter judgment for the arrears of the past eighteen months. When I called Hennepin County Collection Services they told me I had a new social worker, one who was experienced. When I reached her, I heard that she was angry because nothing had been done, that the papers just sat there, and she had been told that something would be done by April 28, 1992. A chip of faith entered me, and I sensed I was to praise and thank the Lord. It was done. So by faith, I cancelled the judgment. On April 28, after leaving cell group—where I told them of my prayer concern and my reason for thanksgiving—in prayer this came forth: "Barbara, this time has been a time of grace for John. Now it is a time of justice. God has been the Judge in this case and has ordered this." John died six months later.

God is faithful. I trust Him. I believe that as I yield to His reign in my life, His faith through me will permit me to take further steps of faith toward the unseen goal of having finances for the missions He calls me to.

CHAPTER 8

Personal Leadership Involvement

May 1993

I 'LL CHOOSE TO start this chapter with events in high school, where I made good enough grades to enter Northwestern University in Evanston, Illinois. In high school and college, however, it was my social leadership that flourished. I was in several social concern clubs and was an officer in each of them, as well as president of our church club, although I was not yet a Christian. During college two leadership roles stood out for me: as an officer in my sorority and my three-year involvement of singing and dancing in our annual variety show (a really big achievement over many contenders).

I graduated as a teacher because of the great concern I felt during an inner-city project with six- through nine-year-olds when I was just sixteen. During the years following graduation from Northwestern University I taught school for a few years, then had my family and moved a lot. I was involved for seventeen years in the Service Club of Chicago, two years of which I was the secretary of the one hundred and fifty thousand dollar annual budget. I was president of my sorority alumni at the time of my husband's death. After being widowed, I went back to work on my master's in education and went to work as a teacher of accelerated third graders. Then I married John and moved to Minnesota. I substitute taught for seven years in Edina and at Breck School and was president of the women of my Episcopal church for two years. After accepting Jesus Christ as my Savior and Lord I began a seven-year involvement with Cursillo, holding many leadership roles, the most significant being the rector (in charge of a team of fifty).

We hosted thirty-six women for the weekend retreat, working alongside the priests, who gave spiritual direction. In preparation for the role of Cursillo rector, I read J. Oswald Sander's book *Spiritual Leadership*, and the next year while going with several others to a weekly Bible study at Stillwater Prison I gave that book to one of the prisoners, along with other books, like *The Hiding Place*. Each week the prisoner would tell me about what he had just read, and upon his release he was one of the few who "made it" on the outside. Praise God! We continued meeting weekly at Stillwater for three years.

Feeling the need for fitness in dealing with the great amount of grief, having lost two more members of my family, I trained at Colonial Church of Edina and became certified to teach aerobic fitness, which I did three times a week for the next six years. I was asked to give a lay sermon from the pulpit one Sunday, which I did on Jesus' power in my life as I was recovering from grief.

Then I laid down teaching and went into the role of church secretary, first at Colonial; then for Dr. Bill Starr, who was freshly retired from having been president of Young Life; and then at Antioch Church. During this time I also went through several counselor training years and co-facilitated a grief group at Colonial. Since then I have been working part time at Antioch and continuing to work in the counseling area through Love Lines and Prayer Lines and, lastly, the grief group at Antioch. I also began four years at Antioch Christian Training School International (ACTS).

When I left for mission to Hong Kong and returned six weeks later in 1990 there were no more counseling groups. It was painful to see the counseling dream die when they let the counseling minister go, but the hardest for me was that when the counseling was being resurrected again, I was not invited to be part of it. Of all the grief I have borne, that one hurt the most, because I felt I was safe at Antioch and protected while going through a horrendous divorce. But it was the watchman who wounded me (Song of Sol. 5:7). I have been mending ever since.

I took a step of faith to say to my pastor in Florida that I sensed that I was receiving a new name, Caleb, and at my age I was "preparing to take the land," although

I didn't know why. Charles Carrin told me of a vision he had had of the name Jephunneh before his eyes. He looked it up in Numbers 13:6 and realized that he was to be a Caleb trainer, and announced that to me. I burst into tears, grateful that I had spoken the "silly words" that were on my heart. (See "The Caleb Journey" of intercession, Chapter 2.) This journey also was included in a chapter in Len LeSourd's book on intercession, *Touching the Heart of God*.

During these years of pain I was praising God on many journeys alone in my car, covering twenty-four states. I found myself praying in the Spirit and doing spiritual warfare, claiming the territory each mile for Jesus and praying for revival in the hearts of the people. The intercession was breaking the strongholds!

Currently, the role for me has not been leadership, except in the counseling field. I have been a receptionist, a server, and a learner. I see it as being in discipleship. I know that every great leader is a server, so I know this period has been preparation for leadership, the way God called me to it, not by my own works, as in the past, or my attempts to be a worker in the kingdom, like in Cursillo or heading up the church women. I am learning the tools in ACTS to continue learning all of my days, that I may be self-disciplined, as I learned from reading Richard Foster's classic, *Celebration of Discipline*, fifteen years ago. I'm to be delighting in the law of the Lord and meditating on it (Ps. 1:1–3), searching for wisdom and understanding (Prov. 3:13). I'm to obey what I meditate on (Josh. 1:7–8), and I'm to continue in His Word and know the truth. I am set free (John 8:31–32), and teaching this truth to others is making disciples of them (Matt. 28:19).

Connecting these leadership roles I have had over the years to my call to the Jews is what I will attempt now. I was drawn to Jews as a child with my dad working for a Jewish boss. I remember how agonized I was at age thirteen to read about the death camp gassings on the front page of the *Chicago Tribune*. I remember vividly reading the book *Exodus* by Leon Uris and seeing the movie (made in 1960). I visited the Holy Land in 1980 and felt like a pilgrim, and I *knew* I would return. I read the book *Exodus II* by Steve Lightle in 1984 and received a call to bring them home to Israel. That vision has never left me, although in 1984 there was no evidence that this was actually going to happen.

In 1991, while in Russia just after the Coup, I began to see signs of the Exodus II actually happening, but there have been so many interruptions to plans and delays that I also see the hand of the enemy in trying to thwart God's plans. I have built up a library of books on the related issues.

For the future I see not much light yet, but I trust that I have gotten to know Him more, and I am more at rest with letting the future come to me one small step at a time, as Caleb did. I don't know yet if I will be assigned a plane load of Jews or a lodge full of Jews or a bus or a car full, or even just one in each hand—whether it will be in

Belarus or Siberia or Alaska, Minnesota or Florida—but I know it will come to pass. In the meantime I have been taking a weekly Bible study course every Sunday afternoon for a year by Zola Levitt and Dr. Jeffrey Seif, and a discussion led by Rabbi Ed Rothman. I hope to go to Israel for the Feast this fall of 1993, staying at the House of Prayer for all Nations.

CHAPTER 9

Journeys to Israel

1980–1995

THE FIRST TIME I went to Israel was with a group of thirty-three, mostly from Saint Stephen's church in Edina, Minnesota. The year was 1980, and sterling silver was at a mega high. I had candelabra and serving dishes in abundance after Mom's death. I checked on whether or not my children were interested in keeping the silver. Then a friend and I took the silver to a dealer. I got sixteen hundred dollars, which was exactly what I needed for a sixteen-day, very well-planned trip to the Holy Land. We took Royal Jordanian Air to Amman and on to Jericho, where we saw the lushness of date palms, fruits, and flowers over against the barren desert dryness—and suspicious looks of the Arabs, even on our side trip to Petra.

Our trip then headed north to the Lebanon border (where the shelling was in the 2006 war), then to Galilee, and down the Mediterranean coast to Haifa and Tel

Aviv. Here I learned that Ronald Reagan had become our new president! We continued south all the way to Arad and Beer Sheva, then to the copper mines and the Negev desert lands into Eilat in time for Shabbat (when every store closes and all traffic stops). We relaxed on the Sabbath at the aquarium on the Red Sea and swam. I was stung by something, but our doctor-traveler patched me up.

The next day we headed up the King's Highway to Jerusalem for five days. My favorite spot was Nof Ginosar Kibbutz. We stayed one night at the Sea of Galilee. I stayed awake all night praying for everyone I knew, looking and listening to the water. I realized then that I was not a tourist but a pilgrim, and I had a sense of assurance that I would be back again in the Land.

It took thirteen years, dotted with short-term mission trips to Monterrey, Mexico; Hong Kong; China; Russia; and several European countries. These trips began in 1983 with the call God gave me when I read *Exodus II.* Even during the four years of Bible college, interspersed in the mission years, all my papers were about Israel.

In 1993, a month before graduation, I had another short God encounter. At 7:00 a.m. I heard, "Barbara, what do you want?" I poured out with, "Oh Lord, I know what I want. I want to go to Israel, to stay at the House of Prayer for All Nations on the Mount of Olives for forty days and forty nights. I want to walk into the city daily and pray in the *souks*, on the ramparts, and throughout the Old City." There was no response, until the next morning at

7:00 a.m.: "Call Jerusalem." I did, even though I'd never called overseas before, and I spoke with the secretary at the House of Prayer for All Nations, who said it would be very busy because of the Feast of Tabernacles, and they had Russian pastors coming. My response was, having been in Russia for two weeks in 1991, "That's just whom I am to meet with."

"Well," she responded, "since you are only one person we will take you—and if it gets too busy, we will move you to the Mount of Olives Hotel." I never had to move.

It was an incredible six weeks of living with people from fourteen different countries, praying in our chapel daily (my time was 9:00 p.m. to midnight). When it was time for the eight-day Feast of Tabernacles, I participated and also made application to work as a volunteer in 1994 and stay at the housing for International Christian Embassy Jerusalem (ICEJ). I was accepted.

In 1994 my Minnesota prayer group had a pre-Israel trip to Sweden, a place on the Baltic Sea where we stayed in a camp-like setting. This is the place where the Jews would come for refuge when they poured out of Russia on their way "home" to Israel. We prayed many times there, then took the train to Amsterdam and did the same there, staying in Harlem and going to Anne Frank's home, and to Corrie ten Boom's as well. (Corrie ten Boom is my heroine.) We battled a lot of spiritual darkness in this liberal city. Everything was permissible there—pornography, drugs, prostitution, homosexuality; you name it. It was hard to trust anyone. I had been prayed for at my Florida church, so I was able to cut right through the spiritual muddle.

My time with ICEJ was a true blessing. We were housed right across the street from Yad Vashem, the Holocaust Memorial. I spent many afternoons there. During the feast we had a gathering with many survivors, and several German Christians in our group asked forgiveness, and many of us prayed with them and for them. I have a video of this. The pageantry of the feast was awesome. We went parading through Jerusalem with banners of the twelve tribes of Israel, and each country in attendance (one hundred and four of them) wore their native dress. There were four thousand visitors to the feast. There were many teachings daily, glorious singing in praise and worship, and dancing for King Yeshua.

In 1995 I repeated this scenario, but I had a grander plan—for I had made all the wedding plans for my marriage to journalist and publisher Bob Walker. One week after I returned to Florida, Bob asked me to fly up to Wheaton, and we had a small wedding there. I met all of Windsor Park, and then we drove to Florida for the planned family wedding.

I never expected to go to Israel a fifth time. I had worked as a volunteer for the three feasts in '93, '94, and '95. Bob died in 2008, and we had never made the trip together, although he had gone in ministry four times. So, this was a bonus for me. I had been on the board of the International Fellowship of Christians and Jews (IFCJ) with Bob for fifteen years. It was my last year on the board, and one of the senior board members handed me an envelope with three thousand in cash in it—to buy my ticket and go as the only board member on the Fall 2009 fellowship "Journey Home." We had several staff members going, so I didn't even have to leave O'Hare alone. I got a wheelchair and joined the group all the way to Ben Gurion in Israel. We had two buses for fifty-three people. With my cane I was able to keep up with all the tourist sites and also, as a board member, enjoy seeing what our contributions bought—from two thousand refurbished bomb shelters in northern Israel; the absorption center we support, where new arrivals begin to learn about their new land and to take Hebrew lessons; to Yad La Kashish, a creative arts center we support that is a life-line to the elderly. (Many members of the creative arts centers were architects, designers, or engineers in their home country and cannot be licensed here.)

Barbara in the prayer shawl purchased at Yad La Kashish.

Another fabulous gift to me was seeing Yemin Orde, a house community for five hundred orphans, near Mt. Carmel. I was overwhelmed by the compassion of the head man, named Barry. Many of these orphans were boy soldiers and saw their parents killed. Barry works with encouragement and love, building them up with a life message that assures them bodily and with words that they will never be abandoned again.

We also had teachings from the rabbi each day, and wonderful fellowship. We had a brilliant guide, a South African woman who has been with Israeli tourism for seventeen years. Does she know her history! I'm content now to pray each day for Israel and not to try to return again. I can picture it all. Hallelujah!

Barbara in Israel - 1980

Barbara with good friends from Minnesota, Zeke and Carrie
Bristol when they made Aliyah to Israel - 1995

Barbara and friends at Qumran, the opening of the Feast of Tabernacles - 1993

Barbara on duty at Feast of Tabernacles - 1993

Barbara and friends met working the Feast International
Christian Embassy Jerusalem - 1993

CHAPTER 10

Memories from Hong Kong

November 1989 to January 1990

P HYLLIS, INA (WHO was born in Denmark), and I began our mission as Bible couriers by flying twenty hours and landing amidst the tall, tall white buildings and water of Hong Kong Harbor. We took a taxi to Mongkok, to a hostel called Promised Land. Instead of the little hotel I pictured, it was mid-block of a tall building with no English labeling outside. Our taxi driver did not speak English either, but led us into a lighted hallway where we spotted the white square sign saying Promised Land Christian Hostel, where we had clean plaster walls, bunk beds, and a shower.

After breakfast we walked to the Revival Church, met our pastor, Dennis Balcombe, a tall, slim blond from Kansas, who spoke fluent Cantonese. We filled out forms for our visas and then had passport photos taken. Two friends of the ministry then helped us with our bags, and we made it to the Mongkok KCR (train). We traveled seven stops north to Fanling. Then a short taxi ride from this station brought us to King's House Ministry, part of Revival China Ministries, serving Hong Kong's 5.5 million people.

Soon we were stashed in our pad, 8A, a *very* nice apartment, which I praise and thank my God in remembrance of. We had three bedrooms, a bath, kitchen, living room, and a rooftop sundeck. The weather was sunny, 68 degrees Fahrenheit, and there was a lot of pollution in the air. We looked out our window down on a huge poinsettia bush.

As we settled in I read Mei Lin Jones's material on this ministry. We found the ministry was eight years old, well-grounded in the Word of God and in self-control and obedience to the Lord and was looking for mature Christians who have overcome, or are in the process of overcoming, the flesh to do the will of the Father. This is serious business. As couriers from fourteen different countries, we carried passports, our immunity from arrest. The native Chinese only have ID cards, and could be detained at the border.

As I said before, the Lord is healing the isolation I have felt, as this is the time my lawyer is awaiting the judgment on my pending divorce. By faith I believe that I am now never alone, never abandoned again. A rejection by man is possible, yes, but never by God. I have that assurance, and I choose to believe it and release any anxiety about the border crossings or being separated from my family and friends.

Wednesday, December 13, 1989

Because of the Tiananmen Square Massacre on June 4, six months ago, we couriers are on single-entry visas. This means we cross the border one day, and the next we intercede for others crossing, from the church, while our visas are renewed. That means three crossings a week, not six.

I woke up this morning at 6 a.m. to a torrent of firecrackers aimed at our flat. It sounded like machine gun fire. Phyllis said it had been going on for an hour. I wonder if the full moon has anything to do with it. We also had seen the small worship cove, so familiar on many streets, all lit with candles and burning incense last night.

I found out with shock that Phyllis and I are each leading a team of three over the border—after only three trips ourselves, and each time to a different border. (We crossed five in all.) Lord! You will be our Guide; no way we can do it without You.

I began to pack—two by two, a Bible, Derek Prince's *Foundations for Faith*, a Bible, *Foundations for Faith*, etc.—putting some in my apron pockets, under my skirt, some in pockets, and in a suitcase to carry through. Soon my two young couriers arrived, both around nineteen, from Australia. We packed up, had a prayer together, and were off for Lo Wu. As we went through customs, all three of us were told to put the bags on the table, purses included.

Lindy had some of hers taken, as did Amantha, and I, but Lindy had some letters to mail in China that they found. One guard was particularly nasty and threatened that if we came through again with printed material we would be punished.

Amantha was given her passport back and got through with about twenty-five small books (often for the three of us it would be seventy-five to one hundred). I made it through with fifteen Bibles and fifteen copies of *Foundations for Faith*. Lindy had a couple in her pockets, and when the guard asked her, she removed them. Then he said he was going to have a woman guard search her more carefully. She was interrogated, and they wrote down the names written on the ten envelopes. And she told them the name where the Bibles and books came from. Her letters were to go to China Radio. This did jeopardize our Bible mission!

We walked about three miles in Red China, looking for a mailbox. Traffic was quickly increasing, being rush hour. After much prayer, we found a mailbox, then stopped to buy a pastry. Amantha took some photos, particularly of the crèche scene near the hotel. What a paradox! A beautiful manger scene in this land of the Dragon!

Only after we cleared the declaration and departure line and arrived into Hong Kong did Amantha see and exclaim that her wallet was missing. A Hong Kong guard asked if he could help, and as we explained he let the two girls go back to search and ask. I waited with the guard and spoke with him about China. I said it was not free like America. I also said I liked Hong Kong very much.

I then asked if he went over to the mainline side, and he said he was not welcome there, particularly in his uniform. He has not been in China. He asked me if the guards spoke English. I said, "Very little."

"Also, they are stern," the guard replied. He looked at me with sad, very kind eyes.

When the girls finally returned, we found out it was true—Amantha's wallet had been taken, probably when she was photographing the crèche, by professional pickpockets, most likely.

It was a trek I shall never forget. The Hong Kong guard gave us our bags and a good-bye with "God bless you."

Phyliss, Ina, and I certainly see two spirits emerging: the gentle, sweet Holy Spirit and the dark Antichrist spirit.

Friday, December 15, 1989

A few months before we left on our journey to China, a pastor-intercessor prayed for us. She told me, "There will be a face, a man, an intimidator," but that I was to "ignore it and move on. No expression, Barbara, as they search. Remember, no hot button."

Ina and I started for our borders at 1:30 after packing. Ina got through, but I was stopped again—the same fierce guard as two days ago. I had been warned earlier in prayer of an intimidator; I was not to be overcome by him, but I did have Bibles and teaching helps taken. I held out for a long time with the two women in the little room, looking into one set of eyes whose owner could not speak English and the other pair of eyes, whose owner mumbled, "You, empty the books from your body."

I did not answer them. Anything would have brought on a barrage of anger. I just looked deeply into their dark eyes, first one woman's, then the other woman's. They were disarmed. But after what seemed an eternity, one went for the evil guard, the intimidator. After many cruel words, including threats of a body search (which I had been told was illegal, as it is not breaking the law to bring in books), I again faced the two women and again the eye contact. I know Jesus' love was coming through to them.

I finally did give up two Bibles and four copies of *Foundations for Faith* in Mandarin. They gave me one Bible back, but no teaching aids. They had not found the six books in the box of crackers, so I did get through with seven, and with Ina's fifty, we checked one full bag at the Century Plaza Hotel. We entered their dining room and ordered coffee and cream cake with melon and kiwi. It was a great experience in a very elegant restaurant. The man at the next table spoke English and was a Hong Kong Chinese who had worked at the US embassy. He had two beautiful young chicks with him, who spent a great deal of time staring at us. It looked like several of the girls in the restaurant were in the seducing business. Our bill was about five dollars each.

It was worth it to catch that glimpse of Red China, and not just the street life—the hordes of people with black hair and black eyes crossing streets and at the border, the beggars, the tangerine sellers who would not take a no but kept following us. It's interesting that there are Red Guards everywhere!

Back at our flat, we may only have a plastic tub to stand in and hand shower, but does it feel good on the dusty, bruised feet! I knew that teaching aerobics and three-mile walks around Lake Harriet were good preparation for this mission. We are easily hoofing three to six miles a day.

At supper Ina told me more of her experiences as a seventeen year old, when the Danish were occupied by the Nazis for five years. She described the SS and the regulars as very different breeds. She fell in love and married a German, who was occupying when she was twenty. She described the way she would answer *"Guten tag"* to the soldier's "Heil Hitler," and when he complained that she was to use the greeting of the occupied, she said she was a Dane and not a German. She also said there was no trouble during the five years, mostly because the Germans respected the Danes as part of their Aryan dream.

As I turn in to my soft bed with a warm water bottle at my feet I am grateful to God for that earlier word about the intimidator. I passed the test! Thank You, Jesus.

Sunday, December 17, 1989

After taking the train (KCR) to Mongkok to the Revival Church for a three-hour blessing of praise and worship in Mandarin and in English, we went up a block to our favorite restaurant, the Riviera, for a set meal of four US dollars—soup, steak, potato, vegetable, roll, coffee, and ice cream.

We then rode the train another direction to Jackie Pullinger's Hang Fook Camp. Jackie is legendary as a young English woman missionary to the down-and-out and opium-drugged who live in the many high-rise buildings with no elevators. She was not present because her mom died yesterday in England. Her good friend, Sister Grace, a missionary from England to Ethiopia, South Africa, and Hong Kong, gave a message that moved me to tears. The service began at four and ended at 7:00 p.m. with four hundred present. I was set free of something, a wound, a pain, a hurt, that was keeping me from walking through the open door of faith. I chose to go for it. For too long I believed I didn't have what it takes. I was afraid. I was dumb. I didn't ask the right questions. I wasn't logical.

So what! I am intuitive, gracious, compassionate, discerning, and understanding. I am hospitable and relate well to people who hurt. I know God loves me, and I am beginning to care about myself again, yet in a different way. No, in a more secure way, at peace and at rest. Thank You, Lord, that You are doing a work in me, a healing work. Thank You for drawing out the pain. Thank You for the intercessors at church here You have given me to help me pray it through.

Tuesday, December 19, 1989

After a busy day, including intercession, we took the train (KCR) to the waterfront and ate at the YMCA. We took some flash photos of the incredible holiday lights, then walked to the cultural center to hear Dr. David Yonggi Cho speak to an audience of two thousand seats. The center was almost full, and what a powerful evening—with a choir of fifty young Chinese and beautiful dancers to drums, guitar, piano, and tambourine. Christmas carols were sung, and worship songs.

Dr. Cho appeared after almost two hours, and his talk was the first in English. He had a Chinese translator. He continued to teach that, "Church growth cannot take place by the power of man, but by His Spirit." God, through Jesus, has made plans for us. He took all our sins, pain, and sickness on Himself two thousand years ago. We walk by faith. We can walk in divine health. Allow yourself to believe. Trust Him. Rest in Him. Cease from your striving. Believe and receive Him. About one thousand came forward. There were words of knowledge and several healings. We were thrilled.

Just as we got up to leave, I looked across at the balcony. My eyes zeroed in on Sister Grace and a friend she was leaning on. I sensed I was to make my way to her through the crowds. When I reached her, she told me she had fallen on her way in and injured one ankle. I asked if I could pray for her. Then I got down on my knees, held her ankle and prayed only in the Spirit. I felt power released into Grace's ankle. I looked up and she had a smile on her face and said, "The pain is gone!" We praised Jesus. What a night. We floated home by train and into bed by midnight.

Monday, December 25, 1989

The paradox—American border patrols search for guns and drugs. China searches for pornographic pictures and Bibles. Security is so tight lately. We sense the need to move the couriers further inland. Lord, You are doing a new thing—we do perceive it! We know we are here because You sent us. We are diversions for the many couriers going deeper into China's heartland.

We left our flat at 10:15 a.m. to go to the train to Hang Fook Camp, where they planned to serve Christmas dinner to one thousand people. We saw Grace, who filled us in on her broken anklebone. She said that when I prayed the pain left—so much so that she slept all night. She went to the hospital in the morning. They set it and kept her overnight. She's getting around just fine. We hugged a few Chinese, said some Merry Christmases and God bless you's and left on the train for TST and the YMCA Christmas Buffet. It cost ten dollars and fifty cents in US currency and consisted of turkey, cranberry, smoked salmon, roast beef, ham, Chinese dishes, many wonderful vegetables, melons, soup, desserts, coffee, croissants, and rolls.

Full then, we wandered and gawked at all the people out shopping on Christmas Day. Every train we rode was packed like sardines in oil.

At 3:00 p.m. we rode the train north to Fanling and our Christmas tea with Curtis and Mei Lin Jones. At least fourteen different countries were present among the couriers—including Romania. The leader of Worldwide Ministries told us the good news of what had just happened in his country, the overthrow of Ceausescu. And we also heard the good news that Noriega is missing (or in hiding) and that we have twenty thousand troops from the US in Panama! Praise God.

Friday, December 29, 1989

I received more scriptures and two words in the night: "I have set before you an open door. Go through. Into a new day. I am with you. He/she whom the Son sets free is free indeed.... Received—turn right. A red light up. You will know." I also received a peace about the divorce trial in Minnesota.

Four-thirty a.m. came early with thirty crows by the rooster. He's getting better. We made the 5:45 a.m. KCR and were just trying to unlock the Revival Church door to go to intercession when Pastor Paul showed up—thank goodness—because if we had gotten in, we would have had the police there for setting off the security alarm!

We heard angelic sounds from the sanctuary. Pastor Dennis was in there, huddled in a corner praying. Another person was singing in the Spirit and calling heaven down. It was just glorious. We had a time of prayer, then boarded the 9 a.m. train for Guangzhou. My partner was Ramsey, aged right between my daughter and son. He stutters, but we still had a great conversation.

The scripture of 2 Timothy 1:7 came forth again, "For God has not given us the spirit of fear, but of power, and love, and self-control." I heard the *power* stressed and not the fear for me. I am not to give away my power. It's His power. I am to wield it "like a sword." As we talked, Ramsey observed, "If the enemy can get a foothold, he will come in and browbeat. Don't turn the other cheek or act like a meek Christian. Act like the world. They are watching for the nice guys but will back off from one who knows who he/she is." Even though this directive seemed to go against Jesus' teaching to turn the other cheek, I felt an immediate sense that Ramsey's observation was under the leading of the Holy Spirit. I knew that this was God's will in this situation, and I knew I must obey in that place, where acting like a meek Christian would have aroused dangerous suspicion.

Well, the moment of truth came. I had "body ministry" on me of twelve books, a cookie tin full, a cracker box full, some with my lunch, and about eight Bibles in a down parka in my big black bag that we refilled to turn in at the hotel, and the rest in my beige carry-on, totaling forty-six. Thirty-one were Bibles and fifteen were Derek Prince materials. I joined up with a tour from Connecticut, got my declaration form filled out and stamped, and by then the tour was gone, so I backed off away from the scanner and backed out for re-entry. I folded the declaration form so the *red stamp* showed and tried another entry point.

The woman guard looked at the stamp and motioned me on—the black bag on the scanner. I couldn't have the beige bag on too, so I tossed the black bag on sideways, and walked out with the beige bag—looking left and seeing no one, looking *right* and seeing another tour. I set the beige bag down (full of Bibles) and went back for the black one, now off the rollers. I grabbed it, turned and walked out, turned *right*, picked up the beige bag—and was home free!

I believe that stamp "received" was the *red stamp*—and the green light for me to go ahead, *turn right*, and get out of there.

I walked the long, long way to the taxi area, knowing all the Bibles under my skirt were not yet removed. So, I stayed near a red guard, walking the same pace but not getting ahead of him. Others also filtered by. I saw a familiar six-foot, two-inch frame smiling. Ramsey and the others were there. All of us got through. Praise God! And with the promise of each Bible being read by one hundred people, we could look forward to twenty-eight thousand people a day getting saved because of all the materials we were able to get through. It was like a *Mission Impossible* episode. I see why. The Lord was preparing me.

We had other tribulations. The hotel we were to take our baggage to would no longer take our baggage if we were not a guest in the hotel. They know what is in the black bags, and it's getting risky, like a net closing. This was our first time in Guangzhou. We found another hotel and checked them. Then I began my adventure.

I was designated to return two and a half hours by local train. Boarding a bus to the train station, a very nice man was next to me who spoke a little English. I felt very safe with one angel assigned to guard me. I had the right money (RMBs), but when I alighted the bus and began going in the wrong direction to the building for my train ticket, he ran after me and got me straight. I had a paper with characters to buy my ticket. A woman helped me this time, knowing some English. It turns out, the RMBs are devalued. They wanted Hong Kong money.

We had assigned seats, and there was a sweet woman across from me who insisted I have one of her tangerines. She could speak no English and I no Chinese, but we had some pleasant glances and a fine handshake two and a half hours later.

The woman I met earlier who knew some English came up again as I left the train. I heard in broken English that she was in the Seventh-Day Adventist Church, born in Beijing, lived in New York for six years, and had been home again in China for one year. She was in Beijing for the massacre on the Square last June 2. She is going back to New York in one month for good, leaving behind her husband and child, who cannot leave (or don't want to). She thought I was a businesswoman. I told her I was a teacher. (My friends later told me I should say, "I'm in my

Father's business.") We parted where she was meeting friends. I choked back tears all the way through customs.

I caught my train home and wobbled into our flat at 6:45 p.m. Ina and Phyllis were waiting for me. We had a weary but joyful and tasty meal in Luen Wo. I do believe the day of prayer and fasting had a lot to do with this major victory in the Spirit realm.

Sunday, December 31, 1989

We took the 10:30 a.m. train to Kowloon Tong to have more visa photos taken. Then we hopped on the KCR to Mongkok and made the three-block walk to the church just in time to begin the 11:00 to 2:00 service. Thank You, Lord, for the wonderful worship and great message on fruitfulness by the brother from Romania.

We ate a fine prix fixe lunch at the Ruby restaurant, and Sarai Lu from Korea (and Washington, DC) joined us. After the meal, Ina and Phyllis went home to Fangling, and Lu and I took the train to Hang Fook Camp for the 4:00 to 7:00 service. The leader had returned from England and gave an inspirational message.

One of her staff came over to us and told me the update on Grace. Two weeks after the break in her ankle she was healed! The cast was off! She went back to South Africa yesterday, and this friend said they were so grateful to God for the prayer promptness with which we responded at the cultural center. She said further that Grace's dad, a soccer player, had broken his ankle in the same spot and had limped the rest of his life.

Not only was the break set for Grace, but after she was kept overnight in the hospital the next morning the set was found to be faulty. The bone was reset correctly—thereby breaking the generational curse and thus the speedy healing of the bones.

I thanked God and chose to set my face toward Him who is eternal, to be aflame for Him, zealous, diligent, and stirring up the gift within me to be "poured out" for Him. The worship songs were in sweet, sweet Spirit, as in Vineyard style, and many of us danced as we did in Israel.

Sarai Lu and I then headed toward Tsim Sha Tsui on the train and walked with New Year's Eve crowds in the rain. We found a Korean restaurant run by a Christian. Lu ordered for us, and the woman at the next table came over. They exchanged emotional words, and she went to the desk and prepaid for our meals. We ate it all, and she said I was a courageous lady. Lu then asked me to pray for her healing, and I did. We had great fun!

We went next door to McDonald's for a cup of coffee and then took the train back to the church in Mongkok by 9:30 p.m. for an all-night prayer meeting—eight hours straight through, by all one hundred and twenty-five of us. That's commitment! The trains stop running at 12:45 a.m. and resume at 5:45 a.m., so we prayer warriors were there to stay—and to ring in 1990.

These believers learned from Yonggi Cho. They mean business. The enemy is out to rob, kill, and destroy, and they are not ignorant of that. We are in a spiritual war.

I loved the prayer meeting but must admit to enjoying the day of sleep following. Ten more days, and I would be going home alone. Ina and Phyllis were staying a month longer. We had four more border adventures together and a visit to a park on Hong Kong Island, across Victoria Harbor by Star Ferry (and Mrs. Field's chocolate chip cookies!), where I sat with a lovely Philippine woman who works for a Hong Kong family. She helped me to identify all the people passing by, as to country, particularly the Asians.

I was teary when I left my two friends at the airport to board an eleven-and-a-half-hour flight to Seattle and customs. Then there were two and a half more hours to Minneapolis. I kissed the ground of the USA when I deplaned. Marvelous memories!

Ina, Barbara, and Daniel

Barbara, Phyllis, and Sarai

Barbara, Phyllis, and Ina

CHAPTER 11

Mission to Russia

1991

PART ONE

I BEGIN BY PRAISING God—we are in Moscow! I will attempt to journal, even though I am riding a moving bus. I will begin with the events that preceded our arrival—the five changes in our plans before our visas came (to minister in the name of the Lord). There was a delay of two weeks, forgetting our actual departure week. When we had bought our tickets, the Russian coup had happened. Gorbachev stepped down, and Yeltsin took over. How difficult it was to believe by faith that we were going, and that we were in the Lord's timing!

Our actual take-off from Minneapolis to Chicago was at noon on September 24, 1991, and we had been on the way until 10:00 p.m. on the twenty-fifth. On the Alitalia flight, we were served a lovely meal, followed by two movies. I was also in the midst of an exciting novel—number one of the Zion Covenant series, *Vienna Prelude*, by Bodie and Brock Thoene. The plane rides were gentle, even though long.

I did remove my contacts after only twelve hours because of the dry air. My eyes became more and more sensitive, until flying over the Mediterranean from Rome to Milan I could not look at the brightness out of the plane window. I took drops in each eye and took authority over this infirmity.

We were to declare all of what we brought with us at customs, and the forms were written in Russian and French. My college French helped a little, but so did a kind business man, who I believed God placed for me. We got our luggage and boxes through customs without much incidence, aside from the fact that Duane and Gary had to count out their money for the agent.

We were then met by Georgi and the men who had arranged our hotels at thirty dollars a night. We also met Andreyev and Ivan, the Jewish gypsy who has booked us into Vitebsk and who said we cannot stay in our Moscow hotel, where we were booked throughout the mission, because we are due for ministry at 2:00 p.m. tomorrow in Vitebsk, which is six to eight hours away. We need to be there tonight, so we ride all night!

We were each given red carnations, Karen, Andrea, and me. Then Constantine joined us. He spoke very good English and was a fountain of knowledge as we all finally got our act together.

After much debate and discussion and procuring a driver for the third car for the long drive ahead, I ended up riding in the big bus with Karen and two Russian drivers (non-English speaking) and all the luggage.

We started out finally by driving to Moscow. The evening was lovely, with almost a full moon, about sixty-five degrees, and beautiful trees turning yellow. We arrived at 9:00 p.m., and McDonald's closes at 10:00 p.m. We hoped to get ten burgers and fries and continue to drive, but it was not to be. The line was ten deep all the way around the park. Andrea did get a photo. The rest of us had our cameras stashed in the hold of the bus. Cars were parked everywhere with no direction control or parking rules.

We insisted, "No problem missing a meal; let's get going!" After more talking in Russian, (I believe decision making is hard for the two men driving our bus), we started out at 9:30 p.m. with the bus leaving and two cars following right into the gasoline station, where our bus had to fill up.

Moving in front of several trucks, we temporarily lost our two cars. They knew where they were meeting us, but we did not, and our drivers did not speak English!

"Go before us, Lord, and pave the way for a fruitful harvest," I prayed.

The roads were two-lane, with the outer edges of each lane broken pavement, so everyone drove down the center of the road, both ways. Our plan after Vitebsk was to go to Riga, Latvia, and Vilnius, Lithuania, then back to Moscow.

I wanted to get some needed sleep, but when we started driving, the two men turned on the Russian pop radio station loudly. I signaled right away that we wanted to sleep, and they did comply. Thank you, Lord.

PART TWO

In Vitebsk we found the home we were seeking at 4:30 a.m., after a six-hour drive. The lovely family fed us at 5:30 a.m., and Karen, Gary, and I went to sleep at last at 6:30 until noon. We were then served another very special meal of broth with three meatballs, bread, steaming hot mashed potatoes, fish fillets, potato salad, and a delicious beet salad. Following the meal we were taken to the home of Michael for a shower. He and his wife are both doctors and teach at the university in Vitebsk. He told of the privileges of ten meters more of living space for a doctorate degree—fifty-nine meters of apartment space for three people instead of thirty-nine. Michael said that now this privilege is no longer honored. She, as a communist, is frightened that the people will turn on them.

Also, if they are robbed, the government leans more to the robber than the victims. It's better, they say, not to defend your property; it goes against you. It is also possible now for a larger family of seven living in three rooms to say to a family of three, "You have five rooms, and you are only three people. Let us switch," and they would take over our place.

Michael graduated from the university twenty years ago and is an English professor. This is the first time in twenty years he has had opportunity to speak with English-speaking people other than when teaching students, who don't know much about English. He has British English, very proper, and he is an intellectual. He is very interested in Christian ideas and is translating a Darby synopsis of the Bible for Ivan, our translator. He is coming to the meeting we have tonight.

Michael showed us potatoes in piles outside his window. People buy them, dry them, and store them in bins in the basement. This could be a very hard winter, and people have broken in to the basement and taken food—just because they want it. There is no recourse, no protection.

The Jewish man next door and his family are moving to Israel. I asked if this friend of ten years is experiencing persecution, and he said not yet. Michael is very interested in ideas of Christianity, but his communist wife is not. He looked at my NKJV Bible. I told him about the NASB, NIV, and the Amplified as well. (We didn't have MEV, NLT, and ESV yet.)

I never did take the time for the shower, only to use the toilet. Our hosts have only an outside toilet and no shower at all. They use the kitchen sink to wash.

When Nadia came home we had coffee then joined the group waiting to take us to the artist Marc Chagalls's home. Other companions were Boris, a new but hidden believer; a newspaper editor, Sergei, who interviewed Duane on tape; and Michael, a Jewish photographer and a new believer.

At 6:00 p.m. we stopped in a café for a lemon drink, open-faced ham sandwich, brioche, and espresso and began to make plans for tonight's meeting at 7:00 p.m.

At the Chagall home I saw some of the busts he sculpted and a bronze statue of him sitting with an inspired look and an angel hovering over him. I was very moved by this.

Ivan had all five of us on stage at the seven o'clock meeting. The theatre-style meeting room was three-quarters full, about one hundred and fifty people. It was touching to see so many faces I had met sitting in the audience. On stage was a rabbi who is orthodox but also believes in Hari Krishna and another Jew who knows the Bible but cannot dilute his Jewishness with Yeshua. It was a very strong debate. After opening prayer and some angelic choir singing a capella we began to share, beginning with me. Ivan translated. I shared as the Spirit directed of my conversion experience while in the grief of losing my firstborn son and my mother, my best friend. I also shared my burden for the Jews over the past seven years, that they are now to return to Israel (make Aliyah), and why believing in Yeshua is important. The rabbi was there, as were our hosts and Michael.

Sharing next were Andrea, Karen, and Gary, then another two choir selections that sent me to the heav-enlies. Duane then began with the simple gospel, Ivan translating. It was very moving. A man and woman came forward for salvation prayer.

We broke for ten minutes and then returned to our

seats for questions from the crowd who remained. I spoke to the woman who became born-again. She is a teacher and was very moved by my testimony. After an hour of questions and some answers by Pentecostals in the group as well as ourselves, we closed with prayer.

On my way out I encountered Michael. I asked how he enjoyed the evening, and he began to pour out his soul—that he was very moved by my sharing, that I looked just like his mother, and that she had been gone about twenty years, and he missed her. We embraced with kisses on both cheeks. Then he said, "I almost converted this night." We talked of my return, and he said he would read and be ready for next time. I often have thought of him, wept, and interceded—and also for the family.

Waiting at the host home was a lovely supper of beet salad, cheese, and butter on bread, liver pate, melon, and cookies with tea. We talked until 12:30 a.m., Georgi translating. Olga asked me to take a package to a friend in Minnesota. She then told of her father who was a pastor during Stalin's days (1937), and was arrested, imprisoned, and died. She was ten years old, four years older than me. A very sad moment of recollection. They asked me if I knew about the KGB. I told them about the counterpart of the PSB in China, and of Daniel in Romania. I also told them of the book I am reading now, years 1937–1938 in Germany and Austria in the *Zion Covenant*. I am grateful I am reading the number one book in the series "for such a time as this" (Esther 4:14).

PART THREE

I arose at 6:45 a.m. after a few hours of sleep and tearful intercession. I had ironed my travel skirt before going to sleep. Irenie showed me which conversion plug of mine was correct. It worked well. I repacked, setting aside the beige mission jacket, two sweaters, blouse, and purple wool skirt for Irenie, crayons and coloring books for Eric and his sister, nylons and babushka for Olga, and also soaps, shaving lotion, and aspirin.

At breakfast we were served tea and more of that wonderful beet salad, open sandwiches, and stuffed blintzes—all delicious.

We left at 8:15 a.m. with Andreyev, Georgi, and Dimitri to pick up the other four with all our luggage, and we began the journey to Kobrin, going through Minsk, Byelorussia. We made a gas stop at ten o'clock and ate fruit soup, meat, and potato-pea soup.

We traveled through eight hours of countryside, seeing collective farms and fields where potatoes had already been harvested. We passed trucks and farm equipment that do not look like International Harvester or John Deere. The aspens are turning yellow. I see no oaks or maple trees. The color was not bright like in America because of the proximity to the accident at Chernobyl.

They cannot buy building materials here. There are long lines to buy everything. They cannot buy a car here now. Three years ago they could buy a car in formerly East Germany for ten thousand rubles. Now that car would cost fifty thousand rubles. Andreyev built his house for fifteen thousand rubles four years ago. Today it would cost two hundred thousand to three hundred thousand rubles.

We arrived at 7:00 p.m. to Andreyev's home and met his lovely wife, Oksana, and their two and a half year old son. Andreyev showed us his beautiful new home— floors of hardwood and inlaid ceilings. It had a large-sized living room, kitchen, and a bath with an inside toilet on the first floor. A family and TV room, and three bedrooms, were on the second floor, plus a balcony.

On Saturday, a rainy day, after eating tomatoes, onions, and sour cream, bread with strawberry jam, tea, coffee, cookies, and cake, we began our adventure to Brest near the Polish border. There were nine of us in the rain. We took in the Fortress, a place of reverence for the Russian people, where they lost to the Nazis in 1941. The Germans destroyed it. We saw the ruins and the amazing stone monument they carved, plus the eternal flame and names of the people slain. We walked about four miles.

The rain was just letting up as we drove into Brest to look for a restaurant to eat before our five o'clock meeting with the Jewish Culture group. There was a long line, as with everything, so Andreyev called a Pentecostal brother to feed us. We went to his home, home to an artist and his parents. There, the artist gave us some of his small paintings, and they provided us a meal of hot tea, cole-slaw, and tomatoes, cheese and bread, as we happily ate around the kitchen table and left in a half hour for our meeting in town.

We were greeted by the Jewish Culture group president and about twenty others. It was very interesting to watch their faces from the front of the room as we shared our vision with them—that we love them, that we are telling them to leave Belarus for Israel. They would like to sell their flats, which the government has recently given them permission to own (after seventy-four years of totalitarianism). They would use the money to leave and to take to Israel. We could see, as the meeting progressed, how they began to trust us, open up, and speak out with questions. At the end of the meeting they were eager to write their names to receive Bibles and more information. The leader will contact other cities and arrange a larger group, and we are invited to stay in their homes the next time. I was in tears at least three times during the meeting.

We drove home to a dinner awaiting us at Andreyev's home. Andreyev's sister made Russian cake and served cabbage rolls, beets, slaw, tomatoes, and caviar, mashed potatoes, cheese, apples, Jell-O, and coffee. Oksana sang for us, with Andreyev on accordion. I had six hours rest that night but didn't sleep at all.

After a breakfast of bread, cheese, butter, jam, and coffee, this Sunday morning we left for the Pentecostal underground church—a meeting in one home. The furniture had been cleared out, and benches were placed in rows. The women, about sixty of them, faced a smaller number of men. Every seat was taken, except one bench by the center table where all five of us sat, plus Claudia, the translator we had last night with the Jewish Culture group.

The singing was incredible. Many songs. The Scriptures were read before the three sermons began. There were fifteen to twenty men standing outside with tape-recorders. The Belarusian pastor spoke, then Gary, then Duane, both pastors. We sang "Spirit of the Living God" and "Alleluia." We were no match for their hearty voices, but what a memorable experience. This was the first time many of them have *seen* Americans. We had to wear scarves, but gauze ones with gold threads—not ours!

I watched their faces. They watched mine. We cried many times. There were over one hundred and forty adults inside and outside that small house. The pastor is sixty-eight. He wept many tears out of red-rimmed eyes. When he was twenty, a believer for one year, he was taken by the Germans with four others. People wrote to spare his life, for he was a good man. They let him go—God's provision!

We went to Georgi's for a special buffet lunch like before, then took our warm coats. The weather was sunny, windy, and sixty-two degrees, but we were going to be in an open stadium holding four thousand people to witness the first open-air crusade held at Kobrin—ever! The sound of the music Georgi organized was wonderful. The people poured in, many walking toward the sound. The stadium filled up, standing room only, and we were awestruck.

Again, there were three sermons. Gary and Duane

were translated by Claudia, a believer. I gave her my beige raincoat. When the call was given for salvation, first by Duane, then by the Belarusian pastor (in threadbare slacks too long for him), the people began to come forward from behind us at the west end of the grounds, and the swell increased all around us. In moments the stands were almost empty, as three thousand of the four thousand came forward for salvation! Georgi, when first renting the stadium in Kobrin, thought maybe it would fill with four thousand and that maybe three hundred to four hundred would come forward. What a miracle it was when three thousand of those gathered came forward for salvation that day, and the other one thousand, already Christians, came forward for healing.

Then we began handing out Bibles and tracts. We gave away everything we had. We also gave an invitation to return to the club Monday evening to ask questions after being saved. We will see how many show up.

Duane was very grateful for Claudia's help in translating as he was laying hands on for healing and salvation for two hours. Gary, Karen, and I were swamped by the new believers with children wanting autographs in their Bibles. I saw and hugged and kissed a number of faces I shall never forget!

Andreyev told us that many, many people came up to him at the stadium and asked what we Americans thought of them. He answered for us that "We liked them real good!"

There are memories we shall never forget. This is the

first time an open-air program for the Christian message has been given, ever. And we are the first Americans to partake, ever! People stare at us. They are not impolite. Many are grateful.

We returned at 8:00 p.m. for more good food, and I slept for ten hours.

PART FOUR

I arose at 8:00 a.m. and took a delightful shower and washed my hair. It was the first time in a week. We had breakfast downstairs in the apartment of Lubka and Dmitri Nikolai. They served us real potato pancakes with sour cream, bread, fish paste, vegetable chunks, apple juice, and coffee. Delicious! The eight glasses were all new, with their labels on.

After a time to relax, I tried to catch up with this journal and also to talk with Pastor Duane about his ministry call, and the narrow road of faith and obedience it has been for him since 1976. It is hard for many Christians to walk the deeper walk. The day of the big preacher is fading into more team ministry today. Thank goodness for my experiences in Minnesota with Charles and Frances Hunter and Phil Buechler, and in Florida with Charles Carrin.

We three ladies took a walk into town with Georgi to buy a few things. I bought a Christmas runner, two puppets, some blocks with the Russian alphabet on them, and a hand-knit hat, which was only seventy-five cents.

Upon our return, you guessed it, we ate again, in

Lubka and Dmitri's flat, with the four Byelorussian pastors who will do a deliverance of evil spirits out of a young girl. (True, I have seen many deliverances. We have an evil enemy who wants to rob, kill, and destroy us [John 10:10].)

We were served borscht made with spinach, sausage, and Havarti cheese, bread, mashed potatoes, tomato, onion, cucumber salad, carbonated drinks, coffee, cookie, and jelly roll.

Tonight was a 7:00 p.m. meeting of the new believers at the club. One pastor talked for fifty-five minutes. I'm so glad we three ladies did not sit up front. There was no Russian translator. I thought it was to be a meeting for new believers to ask questions. Finally they got their chance.

The choir sang three times. I felt sorry for them having to stand the whole two hours. We meet again tomorrow night to begin their education. Many are tired, having worked all day until 5:00 or 5:30 p.m.

Georgi did a fine job of translating for the two short talks of Duane and Gary. Several came forward for Bibles again tonight. We returned to Lubka and Dmitri's for Russian cake, bread, jam, coleslaw, cherry juice, and noodles with gravy.

I finished reading my *Zion Covenant* at 1:15 a.m. and slept until 9:00 a.m., dressed, had breakfast at Lubka's, and relaxed a while. Then we rode to an army/air force surplus store, where we saw a few basics of clothing and paper goods, not much of anything. And the grocery side of the store had lines to buy fish, eggs, and chicken.

We then went to a little shop, the Dayton's department store of Belarus, where I found tablecloths for Lauri and Maggie. Now I just need two dolls in Brest tomorrow.

Home again, we put on our work skirts to build the new upper underground church. Dmitri, Georgi, and then Andreyev came with his supervisor, who is also a Christian. We helped shovel sawdust, mix it with a plaster or cement-like mixture, fill buckets, and haul them to those on the rafters. The bucketfuls were dumped into the space between the roof and the tongue-in-groove panels. We got a little dirty but spread great joy. We returned home very hungry. I ate two bowls of borscht, a wonderful salad of tomatoes, onions, peppers, and cucumbers in cream, bread, butter, jam, and sausage rolls.

In about one hour, Andreyev picked us up for the special evening service at the underground church. We hoped for some new believers to come and learn, and we were not disappointed. There were approximately one hundred and eighty at the tiny home, sitting and standing, and others standing outside the two windows. Katrina (not a Christian) was translating and arrived late. Duane, Gary, and Andrea were praying with someone and couldn't find the house, so they were late.

The people looked at their watches. They sang. One man gave the Psalm reading. They sang again and again. The translator came, then the pastors finally. They knew that Katrina was not a believer. She did not know the

terms of the Bible, and kept translating "gods" for "God."
Sitting next to her I kept praying that she would receive
conviction and the desire to be born again.

The service lasted for two hours and then there were
prayers for healing for the next hour. There were several people from different churches there—like Baptist,
Orthodox, and others. After the closing at 10:30 p.m., we
came home to bread, fruit, coffee, and juice. We arose at
7:00 a.m., eating coffee, bread, jam, and fruit. Planning
to leave at 8:00 a.m. for Brest, Andreyev arrived, and we
talked of buying Russian dolls—but Georgi's car needed
a tire. They found one, amazingly, as they are very hard
to find here, as are windshields, furniture, housing parts,
etc. While putting on the tire, Georgi's muffler fell off. It
is now 11:30 a.m., and we are still waiting.

Xenia told us through Andreyev that when she was
growing up they had one winter coat for five people.
Andreyev struggles with depression. Although he is a
very funny man with dry humor, he is also sad, grieving,
and caught in a boring role of get up and work, eat, sleep,
up, and work again. Andreyev took today off to drive
with us to Brest. He makes one thousand rubles a month
(thirty dollars), no overtime. He is a construction/house-
builder in the collective. Dmitri, as a fireman, makes fifteen dollars a month, and he has five children. They get
paid once a month.

Soon it was time to eat lunch, so we did, then left at
about 1:15 p.m. and arrived at Brest at about 2:00 p.m., but
the stores are closed for one hour for lunch. We walked

the famous closed-off street for five blocks, passing a long line of ladies outside a department store, and learned they were waiting for a sale on pantyhose.

At 3:00 p.m. we entered a large department store, two stories. It looked good on the outside but was very dark, dim, and dingy on the inside—and not much to buy, even less of what is appealing. They have the basics—colorful men's shorts, many socks, two or three kinds of cologne, a few gift items, lots of plastic soap dishes, some musical equipment, and two kinds of cameras. In another aisle were about fifteen winter women's coats—plum, maroon, black, and medium blue. There were long lines in two or three places, but we couldn't see what they were selling. The salesclerks—one with witchy eye make-up—were sullen, almost rude; they were like that to everyone. Our group—Andreyev, Georgi, Dmitri, Ivan, Michael, and their wives—are not like that. The love of God draws us to each other.

Andreyev has only been studying English for eight months, four hours a week. After more walking we bought a watermelon, drove to the shop to buy our dolls, and headed home. I stayed there and repacked for our four-day trip to Vilnius and Riga. Duane went to sleep, and Karen retired to rest. Dmitri called me to have a dinner with Karen down in his flat of potatoes, fried eggs, and tomatoes.

Talking with Andreyev, he said that one year ago he and Georgi knew nothing about English. I asked him about churches in the small villages. "Are there many? I don't see them?" Andreyev answered, about four or five for one hundred villages. When I asked about how many underground churches, he said, "Many." The denominations in Kobrin's city of 50,000 fifty thousand are Baptist, Pentecostal, Catholic, Orthodox, Jesus Only, Seventh-day Adventist, and Jehovah's Witnesses. After more talking we said good night, and I climbed into bed at 1:00 a.m.

PART FIVE

We had a five-hour journey the next day into Lithuania. At the border, Andreyev was asked, "Where is your luggage? Do you have any guns? Drugs?" Andreyev said, "No, we are believers." The guard nodded and smiled. Georgi gave him some tracts, and the guard happily thanked him and walked off.

The country is slightly different, but the relief I see is being able to look at a road sign and begin to sound out the translation—first Lithuanian, then Russian. The houses are bright, neat, clean, well-built, with red tile roofs, not grey as in Russia.

After supper, we went to a prayer meeting in a home— very full. All five of us spoke. Many people hugged and kissed us. Many had prayer requests about losing their jobs. They are afraid. Prices have increased 300 percent in one month.

We had a twelve-hour train ride into Latvia from Lithuania, arriving at 7:30 a.m. We had been without heat for twelve hours. It was colder inside the train than without, which was about 50 degrees Fahrenheit.

Needless to say, we slept in our clothes, with our clothes on, under a sheet and one blanket. I thought of Corrie ten Boom and her World War II challenges.

The travel company that took our money for lodging for thirteen nights met us with a small van, and we toured Riga all day, stopping at 9:00 a.m. at the Hotel Latvia for our free breakfast of appetizers, peas (the potato of Latvia), cheese, bread, baked scrambled eggs, sweet roll, and coffee. We then used the lovely hotel bathroom with toilet paper and paper towels. We continued our tour of Riga in the rain. We saw the beautiful buildings, concert halls, parks, government buildings, and the place where Lenin's statue was removed.

We went into the classic car museum and took pictures of the cars of Khrushchev, Stalin, and Brezhnev with wax models of them either beside the car or in them. Then we headed for the Bay of Riga on the Baltic Sea. We walked for miles it seemed, down the quaint street, looking at stores with very little merchandise. Andreyev could not buy a pair of socks there because he was not a Latvian. We returned to Riga for marinated pork on skewers and dark bread. Everyone loved them except for Duane, who was tired. Then we went to the Communist Party Headquarters, which was now closed, and the streets are now being renamed.

We were taken back to Hotel Latvia for an evening of light supper, a floor show, and dance music. It turned out to be Las Vegas style. Oh well. So the enemy got in a lick! We laughed and remained calm and had a good time.

Soon it was time for the bus to take us back to the train station in the fog to our 11:50 p.m. train for the trip back to Lithuania. Praise God!

And we did sleep! The car was not as cold as the night before, and we arose grubby but ready to face the new day in Lithuania. We went to Georgi's brother Michael's home, where we discovered that Lithuania and Estonia were on our passports, but Latvia was not. Thank you, Lord, for sending the angels to distract the border guards from even checking us!

I praise you, Lord, that young Andrew saw a light in me as I gave my testimony, and he was compelled to come forward to give his life to You. Ivan is an incredible translator. Another lady gave her life to Jesus. She is an English teacher and quite professional, and we heard that the Jews in Vitebsk are all stirred up! Praise the Lord!

We took the rest of our luggage to our hotel here and checked in. The travel agency we paid in Moscow has been very fair to us. We got the van from Moscow to Vitebsk, the three train rides, food at the hotel, showers, and a tour through a castle after a lunch of appetizers, soup, salad, and beef stroganoff.

Karen was not feeling well, and Duane is still on a squeamish stomach. Gary is running in the nose and coughing, and now Georgi and Andreyev started. Please keep us, Lord; we look to You.

We had dinner for eight at a fine old Russian restaurant of smoked salmon, caviar, good bread, two salads, three meats, and veggies to start. Then pork and mushrooms, potato puffs and beets, and a dessert of ice cream. And Dimitri, the tour guide, again picked up the tab, so we feel we did get our money's worth and time redeemed for paying for thirteen hotel rooms we didn't use.

The motel room is comfortable, even if the heat is not on. (I understand there is a shortage of coal for heating.) So we again layer up like I did some nights in Hong Kong. I had a wonderful rest, with two blankets. (My cashmere sweater and long underwear for warmth were left in the suitcase we couldn't bring along.)

We left by 8:30 on Sunday for Michael's and a wonderful breakfast. We left our luggage there and were taken to church—a Lithuanian/Russian/Baptist/Pentecostal church that is registered under the name Baptist. Nicolas was a good interpreter. I talked for ten minutes about Israel and the call to the Jews, and Duane gave the sermon. We had a long communion service with Ivan in command. After the two and a half hour service we gathered outside. Duane and Ivan talked with a Jewish man who wants to emigrate, but his wife is Lithuanian and doesn't want to go. While waiting for them I greeted and hugged and kissed many. Georgi brought into our group a former KGB officer, retired, who is now a Christian. As I was reaching to shake his hand, a bee stung me on the back of my neck! My neck began really hurting. I did ask for prayer and believed that the poison was draining out of me. I endured the day.

After a fine dinner it was time to pack the two cars and take off for the four o'clock meeting at the Union, the registered, formerly underground, Pentecostal church whose prayer meeting we had been at four days ago when all five of us spoke. The music was great. It was so wonderful to see such zealous young Christians. The young pastor just glows with the joy of the Spirit.

About seventy-five to one hundred people came forward for salvation. One young man who spoke English said, "It is a miracle."

Tonight about one hundred came forward for prayers for healing. We only had the union for two hours, so we had to shorten the prayers amidst lights flashing. I met a messianic Jew who is trying to emigrate with her blind mother. They need to make their decision within two weeks.

We closed up the place and headed home to Kobrin, four hours away in Belarus. I borrowed Duane's parka, soft around my neck yet a support for the temporary ache and paralysis of the neck muscle. It was quite a ride in Georgi's car, a two-door with poor shocks over incredibly bad Russian roads—narrow, lumpy, with debris on them like bricks. Road-building is done, but with no warnings or detours. The angels of all of us were hard at work this evening. We arrived in Kobrin at 11:30 pm. Xenia had chicken and vegetable soup, coleslaw, baked apples, and bread. And we all crashed for the night in the beds she had already made up.

PART SIX

I did not set an alarm, knowing this was a day of rest. I woke up at 8:00 a.m. and arose to shower and wash my hair, but there is no pressure, so the gas won't kick on to heat the hot water. Andrea and I will wait out another day. We have the eleven-hour train ride from Brest to Moscow tonight, getting in at 11:00 a.m. tomorrow. We planned to tour Red Square, etc., and get to the airport by 4:30 p.m. for departure to Rome, leaving at 6:00 p.m. and arriving at our hotel in Rome at 11:00 p.m.—we thought.

We feasted on hot potato pancakes with sour cream. All the relatives began arriving. Andrea and I were trying to pack for the journey home, taking to Rome only our carry-on and checking the rest of our luggage to go straight through from Moscow to Minnesota. Duane, Andrea, and Georgi left to pray for a woman who has a spirit of fear and whose children are always sick. I really wanted to go with them, but I am here writing with my left hand as several non-English-speaking natives look on.

Xenia gave me her precious three-part Russian doll from her cabinet. No one can buy them anymore. Andreyev gave me a beautiful book of nature. I shall enjoy it later. As I write today, they are preparing a major dinner/going away festive meal. I will try to name the goodies arriving at this table we have set for sixteen: mashed potatoes with carrots and onions on top, meat, shredded beets, tomatoes, cabbage rolls, baked apples, coleslaw, cheese, bread, a homemade torte, and cookies.

After being polite with all the good food, I feel the first upset of the trip. I have given out Pepto-Bismol to others, but I have not used it until now. I praise God for the good health and stamina.

The relatives kept dropping in. We prayed for a family with a Down's child who does not speak. The water pressure came back on, so I took advantage of it and washed my hair. I sat with twenty people and ten children with a wet head.

This is such a loving large family. I have never had this. Xenia has twenty-five grandchildren. We begged off having another meal, and after much dialogue, thanks to Ivan's excellent interpreting, we began to pack the three cars for the trip to Brest. Again we talked and at last boarded the train. It pulled out on time at 10:00 p.m. It is much cleaner than the other trains, and the temperature is comfortable without a coat.

It is hard to believe that twelve days have gone by, and we spent another night on a train (a very nice one). I battled the intestinal bug all night, but with prayer in the Spirit and taking authority, walking in my victory in Christ, I survived the night, and I feel wonderful!

We arrived in Moscow at noon and took all of our bags to the waiting bus with Constantine the driver. We had a controlling woman with red hair who groused, griped, and directed our every move, including the tour of the city.

As Constantine would speak in English, her voice would rise, and we couldn't hear him. Ivan was trying to talk from behind us, but we couldn't hear him either. The louder she got, the more she pointed, usually across my nose. I finally moved to the rear with Ivan, and what he didn't know about I missed—and I didn't care.

We did get to Red Square. This was worth the tour, and the bossy woman did not get off the bus to walk with us. We stayed for the changing of the guard with their high-stepping march. Ivan and I are delighted that we are free to be us instead of the regimental guards. Then with occasional sirens screeching we circled the square and headed out to the international airport.

We made it on time and went through customs in five minutes. The Alitalia check-in had no line. We had hugged and kissed Georgi and Ivan good-bye, much to the pain on the face of the customs man. We are on our way out of the former Soviet Union, now Russia, to freedom once again. This was a hard good-bye. We leave our new friends in confusion, much despair, little hope, except in Jesus, who is the hope of the world.

I sat in my plane seat alone, for my Italian seatmate chose to move back two rows so he could work with head phones on. My meal was delicious—roast beef, asparagus, carrots, salad, roll, cheese, crackers, custard, wine, and coffee. I saw a group of Italians ahead who are enjoying life the world's way and really making fools of themselves, grinning, gregarious, and flirtatious. They think nothing of the no-smoking regulations and are carrying champagne back here from first class. The stewards seem to approve.

I have not reread this journal yet, but some things stand out to me: the smelly bathrooms wherever we were except on Alitalia, the precious and evident love of the Russian people for us, the first Americans to visit these areas in ministry ever, the way our hosts shared their hospitality and all they had (even off their shelves), and the loving relationship of relatives, which I never knew until the joy of knowing and being part of fellowship in God's family. It is incredible how one we are in Christ by the power of the Holy Spirit, regardless of the barriers of language.

PART SEVEN

It may be difficult to chronicle here all that has transpired in the past thirty-six hours. We certainly were coming ripe for an attack of the enemy, for coming out of God's specially prepared days of protection and viewing His harvest in awe to now seeing the humanist world of decadent Rome and the philosophy of Dr. Richard, who was to be our tour guide.

We arrived on time at 11:15 in Rome (12:15 Moscow time), anticipating the next part of our adventure. We waited and waited and yet again waited for our luggage— one and a half hours. It seems the crew was tired. The pilots and stewards left, locking up the plane, including the luggage bay! They had to call technicians to get the electrical power working to open the bay doors to open the luggage.

At one point Duane went up to find our guide, for

we didn't have any advance information on our stop in Rome. An Englishman named Richard met him, carrying a placard of information. Duane came back beaming. At least we had someone awaiting us as soon as we could collect our luggage. We would store our two big bags here and go into Rome with only hand luggage. It could have been checked right through to Minneapolis–St. Paul Airport, but our stop in Rome was over twenty-four hours, so we had to claim it, check it, and recheck it at our ticketing time the next day.

By the time we had everything accounted for and met Richard we had missed the last train into Rome. It cost ninety US dollars for two taxies into Rome, twenty-six kilometers away, so we waited for the next bus, which left at 2:15 a.m., taking us to the station. We still had a taxi ride to the Pensione di Milazzo. Richard said we would have breakfast at 7:30 a.m. before the 8:15 a.m. tour bus picked us up.

We finally bedded down at 3:30 for three hours of sleep. Arising, we were told there was no breakfast at our pensione, so Richard walked us to a pizza storefront for a western breakfast of ham, two fried eggs, bread, and jam. I had a chocolate croissant and cappuccino. While we waited for the food Richard crossed the street to convert twenty US dollars each from us into what he called two thousand lira. He really pocketed three dollars and fifty cents from each of us. He converted the money for our lunch, which we would have to buy after the tour.

Then Richard would take us to the Steps, the Forum,

and a charming little spot for dinner on him. Then we would see the Coliseum at night and more of the fountains. Or so we thought!

Our tour met up with other buses at the Quirinale Gardens and began our four-language tour at 10:00 a.m. Half of it was walking, and I enjoyed it. The guide had excellent comments—brief, because she had to go through four languages each spiel. Richard filled in all the details with endless prattle. He knew quite a bit of history, actually. He gave me the entire history of the Roman Empire, including dates, the popes, etc. My head was swimming. Remember, I was operating on three hours of sleep. He was my seat partner and went on and on. Soon we began to walk down the steps where Mussolini gave his famous speeches to the Trevi Fountain. It had just been restored and was a beautiful sight.

We all took pictures as we walked through ancient Rome—the Parthenon, more fountains, and Navona Square. Later I bought some postcards to see again what I saw. I ran out of film at the Tiber River and Bridge of the Angels, just before entering Vatican City. We had toilet breaks and a time to buy film and gifts before entering St. Peter's Square. I heard an inner voice say, "You don't need to take any more pictures now." I was content. I did not need to chronicle Vatican City on film, or the Coliseum, which we viewed at night.

After a heated discussion during Richard's orations over the blessedness of Mary and the role (or non-role) of Pope Pious in the World War II years—Richard would not listen to truth—we finally agreed to disagree. I really don't remember much about walking amongst the remains of popes and other venerable things under St. Peter's because of our "discussion."

Up from the tombs, we chose not to stand in the long line to ride up to the dome of St. Peter's and climbed the three hundred and twenty-two steps to the top. We were informed that the Sistine Chapel was closed for the afternoon. I was hoping to see the newly reopened chapel after three years of cleaning and restoration, paid for by the Japanese government for the film they did on the chapel. I had wanted to see the hand of God touching man in relation to the whole ceiling, but it was not to be. We did accomplish our mission, though, of placing remembrance stones at the foundation of St. Peter's.

We strolled back to our tour bus in the Italian sunshine and heat of the day, feeling our lack of adequate rest. We made a change of plans for the rest of our day in Rome as we returned to the area of our pensione. Instead of Richard escorting us any longer and our buying lunch, we determined that he would buy us lunch and we would skip supper and turn in early. He also would take us by train to the airport early and, when we had checked in, buy us breakfast.

We had three false stops attempting to buy lunch at 2:00 p.m.—one was too expensive according to Richard, another not right, and finally he determined that we would eat at the train station. Come on now, Richard!

Then we found a little cubby with ten tables and

nestled ourselves in for two sprites each, while Richard had a beer and ordered a liter of white wine. They all ordered lasagna, while I ordered scaloppini alla marsala. We were served the house salad, Duchess potatoes, spinach, delicious mushrooms, and a small loaf of bread each. Dessert was melon and coffee. I was contented. My meal was great!

The other four sat together and talked and also determined their plans from that point on without Richard. I was sitting with him, listening to more of his "intellect." Actually, we got on the subject of his girlfriend being Chinese, and he was able to hear and agree with much of what I shared about Hong Kong and the terrible hunger about spiritual things among the Chinese. I shared about a friend of mine having had acceptances with scholarships to Princeton Seminary, Harvard, and Cambridge. Richard admitted to having his undergraduate and doctoral work done at Cambridge. How can he be so bright and still be the bumbling Inspector Clouseau? Even more, how could he be what Andrea termed "an idiot"? I believe it was more accurately the biblical form of the fool. He was self-serving, prideful, and a know-it-all! He was very opinionated and interrupted a lot. At any rate, when my four friends got up to leave I left with them, and Richard stayed behind to finish his wine and pay his bill.

We decided to walk to the Coliseum, arriving just before sunset. I knew I was in trouble with my feet again. I had punished them for too long with too little rest in between. The Coliseum is awesome. What a price the martyrs paid, and to think that Christianity has survived all that. Many of my friends believe they will be martyred. What is ahead for us? Lord, help us!

We arrived home just before 9:00 p.m., and I showered. We turned in before ten o'clock, having secured a blanket. We left the window open all night to the sounds of Roman life. The alarm was set for 5:30 a.m., and we were ready for it.

Richard had been on reconnaissance, and we were now to take the metro and not the fast train, which he claimed was so good. To make a long, long story short, we switched from metro to fast train, all of which we could do on our own without need of a guide. While claiming our checked baggage, we had to pay eight US dollars per checked bag. Then there were the three Italians who thought they should go through ticketing before us, and one threw a fit! We let them in, and later won the praise of the grateful ticket agent. She was embarrassed but not allowed to take sides.

Finally we booked in, dismissed Richard, and ran for the customs/passport check—and then for the terminal for immediate boarding. So much for that breakfast he was going to buy us. I believe we need refunds from Duane's travel agent.

Our flight, flight 664, was due to leave at 9:40 a.m. We were an hour late. Then one hour into the flight—just after a lovely dinner—we had an emergency. A seventy-five-year-old man went into a seizure and was given oxygen. There was a doctor on board. The stewards laid him on the floor behind Gary and Karen. We flew one hour north of our flight path and made an emergency landing at Reykjavik, Iceland, a place with no trees, for him to be taken to the hospital there. I was in intercession for him.

Then we refueled. A 747 uses an incredible amount of fuel on take-off (more than our steward said he could use in the lifetime of his car). The projected flight time from Iceland to Chicago over New Brunswick is five and a half hours, which brings us into Chicago fifteen minutes after our connecting flight to MSP, so we take another flight. Our Minnesota people will be there to pick us up, and we cannot tell them in Chicago until we go through customs and get the new flight number. We'll be home soon!

Ivan (under lamplight), our gypsy interpreter, Barbara,
with American pastors Gary and Duane - 1991

Barbara with a Russian host family - 1991

Some of the Jewish culture group in Belarus, ready
to make Aliyah to Israel - 1991

CHAPTER 12

Mission to Scandinavia, Western Europe, and Israel: Fifty-Two Days

August–October 1994

THE DAY BEFORE I left for this fifty-two-day mission, August 14, I received a call from an intercessor in Tampa who met me once in Virginia Beach in June. She asked where I was going, and as I named the countries—Denmark, Sweden, Germany, Austria, Switzerland, Holland, and Israel—she kept murmuring in agreement and finally said, "Yes! Those are the nations many of us are being sent to. Although we usually go to Jerusalem first, for there is an anointing there to go out to the nations. This time it is reversed. God is about to pour out great revival upon these nations. This is the *big* one."

This was a confirmation of the steps of faith I had taken to prepare for the journey—applying and receiving acceptance to work at the Feast of Tabernacles in Jerusalem, then receiving a call from one of four intercessors in Minneapolis, who I had prayed with for eight years regarding the release of the Jews to "go home" to Israel, and who said to me, "The time is now! Can you go with us?"

I did take the risk of stepping out in faith, and many doors opened to me. The money for my journey miraculously poured in, and I gratefully boarded the flight for the journey of my life—a most amazing one—because God was in charge of every step of the way, the hard work and the fun.

A specific prayer prayed over me just before I left warned of hindering spirits and perverse spirits on assignment in Germany and in Holland. All else was clear. We did find a heaviness and hindrances in Frankfurt, and also a blatantly perverse area of gay bars and erotica on our city tour. And Frankfurt, we just discovered, is now the new economic and banking capitol of the European Union! The trip to Berlin had to be cancelled.

In Holland, after all the others had flown home, my hostess received a call to come and pray at her friend's home, for the battle was fierce, and she couldn't handle it and at last cried out for help. The husband and father had had several mini-strokes and was not the head of the home. His wife was a Christian but very overprotective yet permissive with the children as they got older. Of the five children, aged twenty-nine to sixteen, only the oldest boy and only girl were clean and clear and living out of the country. The others had gotten into drugs and perversion, even homosexuality and incest! Five women came together in agreement—four Dutch and I—and we did warfare to break the strongholds. Later that afternoon, the twenty-six-year-old son, who had daily come to harass and steal money from them, returned to the home but was soon met by the authorities, who protected the parents.

I praised God for the advance word of warning here in Florida, and for the courage and boldness to do battle with the unseen. What I learned was that the body of Christ is the same when it is one—from every tribe, tongue, and nation. This became even more evident when I arrived in Jerusalem amongst ninety-four nations, who were celebrating the Fall Feast and standing in unity with Israel and God's plan to favor her in these end days.

The director of the International Christian Embassy spoke of members of the embassy as ambassadors, envoys to meet the leaders of other nations—even the ones at enmity with them. As embassy members we also are ambassadors to portray Israel to the churches internationally and sometimes speak prophetically to national leaders.

My two separate experiences in Israel this year were both with many nations. I worked with hostesses and ushers from eleven nations, and when I lived at Halcyon House under Sister Ruth Ward Heflin, I became friends with jewels from Israel—both Arab and Jew—from New Zealand, England, Australia, South Africa, Korea,

Germany, Kenya, Sierra Leone (including the princess and her travelling companion, who I had met last year), Norway, Canada, and the USA.

I learned to live in harmony and peace with many nations, to choose to accept the favor of the Lord, to freely worship Him who is alive in beauty and in holiness, to freely dance before Him and sing and laugh with joy, to believe the vision He has given me for Israel, to proclaim it with my mouth, and to walk it out, knowing that He is with me.

This journey is part of that walk. He is faithful to see us to completion (Phil. 1:6).

Here are some insights on the European spiritual awakening that we were praying for and walking out: that revival will break forth in the Dutch Reformed Churches in South Africa, the USA, and Holland—the places of the windmills—and also in Germany, Austria, and Switzerland. Two days later I heard a prophetic word that revival will sweep Sweden! Praise the Lord! There is yet a greater glory to be revealed, and it will be seen on us. We will live in it, the glory of God. He is making all things new!

There are common elements present.

1. Intercessors see their praying intensified, like travail before birth.

2. Christians are freed from bondage to the clock and begin times of waiting upon God in praise and worship.

3. There is growth of groups with a strong desire to pray.

4. There is a new awareness of sin, leading to repentance and forgiveness.

5. Preparation of the heart in this way leads to renewed joy in knowing Jesus and desire to share Him with others.

There is an air of expectancy over Jerusalem, of a spiritual breakthrough. At least three rabbis have asked a Messianic leader for the baptism of the Holy Spirit, and he has prayed with them, and they have received! And when some Arabs were recently saved, they immediately lost their rage and began to witness to nearby Jews! Praise God, or as the Jews say, "Thanks God!" He is in control, and the time to favor Zion has come!

There were many moments of blessing on this journey. Below are excerpts from my journal notes.

August 15

I cried for joy upon finding that I had been placed in business class on KLM (Royal Dutch Airlines), window seat A-3, for the seven and a half hours to Amsterdam. It was a gift I gratefully received. I even had a seat partner who was a missionary nurse/midwife in a remote part of Kenya.

August 21

I am grateful for the divine opportunity to pray for the dedicated Christian young men in Sweden to empower them for the busy days ahead. Also for the pastor and his wife, newly renewed with hope, that truly this place is "the place where God makes miracles."

August 23

I am grateful for the angelic help along the way in handling our luggage and in finding the right train and seats!

August 27

I am grateful for the incredible blessing of the *Sound of Music* four-hour tour while in Salzburg. The tour host was named Andrew and had a beautiful tenor voice to sing with the soundtrack as we would drive and "climb every mountain."

August 28

I am grateful for the awesome train ride through the Austrian Arlberg and seeing the Swiss mountain lakes.

August 30

I am grateful for the precious two-hour tour of the ten Boom house in Haarlem, Holland, and

the equally moving two hours Marlene and I
spent at the Anne Frank House in Amsterdam.

September 3

I am grateful for a wedding in a castle at
Amerongen, Holland. Pillars of marble with
crowns on the tops and lights extended from
marble arms and hands on each pillar reminded
me that we hold His light out to the world from
our individual pillars, often alone, and in a
corner (holding up the roof), or standing side
by side without touching or speaking to one
another.

September 4

The Lord shone His light upon us as we walked
out onto the battlefield of the tragic Battle of
Arnhem (1944) to the River Rhine. We reclaimed
the land from darkness and death and painful
remembrances after fifty years. I was reminded
of the prophecy given to a church leader that
there will be a new battle plan. Now witnesses
will stand and testify to the victory of Jesus
Christ, bondages will break, and the captives
will be set free!

September 5

I am grateful for answers to prayer for the family
I stayed with in Holland.

September 8

I am grateful for precious time walking among the sheep in the heather, to the shepherd and his dog, reclaiming the land where our paratroopers landed fifty years ago.

September 12

I was dropped off in Jerusalem by a taxi driver at 1:30 a.m., right at the door of my destination at the Heflin home. I was ushered in to the big corner room, the "pink room," to sleep all by myself in a big double bed. I felt like a princess or an ambassador! What a blessing for four days.

September 14

I was given the opportunity to lead people through the Old City to the Western Wall and home again. Thank God for the experiences He gave me last year in getting to know Jerusalem.

September 17–23

I am grateful for precious pilgrimages to Caesarea, Megiddo, Be'it She'an, the Golan, the Galilee—and even a wedding in the ruins of the synagogue of Capernaum, climaxed by a sudden wind and sweet rain over the Sea of Galilee.

September 18–26

I am grateful for moments again and again at Yad Vashem—only a ten-minute walk from our housing for the Feast. I had my picture taken at the tree in memory of Corrie ten Boom, a small tree—for when she died, her tree of remembrance died also. The Children's Memorial was unforgettable, as was the memorial service that the ICEJ held for the first time when Jan Willem of Holland, a German, and a Swiss Christian asked for the forgiveness of the Jews for not standing with them. It was powerful!

September 19

I am grateful for the desert beginning of the Feast of Tabernacles at Qumran. We celebrated the birth of Yeshua in Succoth stall and later the same stall was used tying in to the Feast celebration. Awesome!

September 27

I am grateful for special time with two Jewish young women at the Western Wall during Simcah Torah, alongside the rabbis and faithful, rejoicing in the Law. (See Song of Solomon 1:4.)

September 28–October 4

> I am grateful for the wonderful return to
> Halcyon House, to sleep in the room with angels.
> I sensed them there, but didn't see any.

And there were some attempts by flesh or the enemy
to steal our joy:

August 17

> In Denmark, when Marlene and I went to get her
> luggage, the door was ajar, and her storage locker
> was empty. We had several anxious moments
> until we realized that we were in the next band
> of lockers, and we did both get our luggage! The
> same day, in Sweden, after travelling all day
> by ferry boat, train, and bus, we got to the last
> town and called the house number given to us,
> and there was no answer! The season had ended
> three days before we arrived, and there was now
> only one bus a day to where we were going—and
> we had missed it! Help, Lord! And He did.

August 21

> I was attacked by spirits of rejection and misun-
> derstanding.

August 23

I watched a young woman get robbed, and the robber get away as our train pulled in to Frankfurt at 6:30 a.m. I discerned spirits of materialism and mammon, perversion, and control in Germany. Also I discerned pride in the ethnic areas—Prussians still against those in Bavaria.

August 29

It was a huge spiritual battle to get our sleeping compartment. It seems it was put on the other end of the train. We had to find it because the other train cars are "dropped off" during the night to go other places.

September 3

I had an unusual attack of stomach cramps after enjoying cheese fondue. After a difficult three hours, yet no vomiting, I was again fine.

September 6

I was attacked by a spirit of jealousy and lies. Agree with your adversary quickly, and respond in the opposite spirit. The storm passed, and sweet calm returned.

Earlier that same day there was warfare of being detained by the Dutch traffic police, and a big hickory nut hit Gerda's windshield to divert our attempts to reach our destination to pray and to break perverse spirit strongholds in her friend's house. We had victory with Jesus!

September 10

I had a fast-as-lightning incident with both of my contact lenses ending up in the sink. One caught in the over-flow hole, which Peter retrieved with a Q-tip. Praise God! Also, I discerned, with Solvei and Peter, the perverse spirit of Holland with legalized prostitution, homosexuality, drugs, abortion, and euthanasia. Much harassment!

September 12–15

There is high heat in Jerusalem—four days of 100–105 degree weather, and no one has air-conditioning.

September 15

I found out I have four roommates, not two or three. One in each age level: twenties, thirties, forties, fifties, and me. We did well together!

September 16

An earthquake woke us on our first morning together.

September 30

We encountered more warfare as we went back to the House of Prayer on the Mount of Olives.

October 5

I had to pay a lot for my luggage in storage in Holland. Also, I checked my luggage through with the same tag destination as my first bag tagged at Tel Aviv. I found out at Atlanta, when going through customs, that my two bags were slated to go Baucau, Idaho, or Indonesia (he wasn't sure), but not to Palm Beach International! Without that sharp customs man, I might never have seen my luggage again. Again, victory in Jesus!

This journey was life-changing in me, and certainly unforgettable! Glory to God!

Barbara in Sweden - 1994

Barbara at The Tenboom Clock Shop

Barbara in The Hiding Place - 1994

Crown

"My life is like a weaving between my God and me.
I do not choose the colors, He worketh steadily.
Ofttimes He weaveth sorrow and I in foolish pride,
Forget He see the upper and I the underside."
—CORRIE TEN BOOM, THE HIDING PLACE

Crown

CHAPTER 13

Adventures with Bob

I AM IN A dilemma. I have just read through thirteen years of Christmas letters chronicling the happy and adventurous times married to Bob Walker.

I met Bob in early 1995 when the LeSourds asked us to a church gathering at my condo building. I was teaching at my church, so I would be fifteen minutes late. Sandy said that was fine, and when I appeared in the doorway of the room, Bob saw me and immediately received the words, "There's the woman you are going to marry!" He was shocked at first but got over it, and we dated for ten months and then married at the end of 1995.

He was a perfect helpmate for me—a caring husband yet also a father figure for what I was missing growing up. He was also a father for Lauri and Eric, and also a lively grandfather for my five grands, who were six, six, seven, eight, and nine when we married in 1995.

The wedding ring Bob had made for me is a circle of Hebrew letters in gold saying, "My beloved is mine, and I am his" (Song of Sol. 2:16). I treasure it, and it reminds me daily to pray Psalm 122:6 for the peace of Jerusalem.

My dilemma is that I don't know how to condense the

active lives we lived into a piece for a memoir. Perhaps the ten weddings of children and grandchildren or the two family visits we had at Williamsburg Marriott Timeshare and Washington, D.C., would be a good place to begin. But for the moment I'll focus on the adventures I had with Bob.

When we purchased our timeshare we were given a gift of travel to any place in the world, round-trip. We chose to go to Australia for a couple of reasons. It was the only continent Bob had not visited, and my brother and his wife had moved there the year before. In 2001, we flew to Sydney first and spent eight days in the Sydney Marriott, then flew one way to Melbourne for a nine-day visit with my brother, Larry Melin, and Kim and her family. We then made a side trip of two weeks in New Zealand aboard the *Legend of the Seas*.

And there were more cruises. Bob loved the sea, and I enjoyed taking our luggage aboard and putting it in the closet for the whole cruise—to Alaska aboard the Princess Line in 1996, to the Caribbean in 1998 with a group from our Florida church, and to the mega Wheaton College–sponsored adventure aboard the *Sea Cloud* (a thirty-nine-sail yacht) to the seven churches in Turkey following the travels of Paul in the Aegean Sea in 2003.

Perhaps it was the memories of conferences like the one spent for four days at Billy Graham's "The Cove" in Asheville, North Carolina, in 1997. Then there was a weeklong circle trip by bus through all the parts of Switzerland, followed by the International Leaders for

Discipleship Conference in Eastbourne, England, in 1999, which gave me my first visit to London, the Cotswolds, Stratford-Upon-Avon, Canterbury, and Eastbourne on the English Channel.

All of these adventures were peppered with the work God prepared for us to do, teaching Bible studies either in Florida or here in Wheaton. Even though Bob was retired he exclaimed, "We're not retired; we're refired into the ways of God." And, God blessed us "real good"!

The Walkers in Zermatt, Switzerland - 1999

Bob and Barbara in the Cotswolds - 1999

Bob and Barbara in Switzerland - 1999

Bob and Barbara alongside the Sea Cloud at the harbor near Ephesus - 2003

The Walkers on the trail of the Seven Churches - Turkey, 2003

Bob and Barbara honeymooning in Alaska - 1996

CHAPTER 14

My Spiritual Journey with Reflections on the Song of Solomon

A S I MATURED in Christ, I became able to understand the Song of Solomon at so much more than face value. The Holy Spirit began to reveal the depth of His love and His plan for me through that book, and as He did, I learned more about my God and my role as His bride. Though it took years for me to understand the fullness of relationship God wanted me to share with Him, as I look back on those first decades I spent with the Lord I am able to see how beautifully He wooed me and sang over me. I now know that my testimony is really our love story, for "I am my beloved's and my beloved is mine" (Song of Sol. 6:3).

In the paragraphs below I summarize how I came to know and walk intimately with the Lord. At the end of each major era of my life I have included a reference from the Song of Solomon that perfectly represents that season. I pray that it causes you to reflect on how God has wooed and is still wooing you, His beloved. If at the end of this chapter you are still unsure of His love, I encourage you to look up those scriptures and to seek out a recording of Kari Jobe's worship song "My Beloved." May the Holy Spirit speak to you through them as He did to me.

In deep grief over the death by suicide of my eldest child at sixteen and the loss of my beloved mother to cancer twenty days later, I wailed in pain, and no one seemed to understand. I was widowed seven years earlier by a car accident, and at that time many seemed unable to relate. But, four months into this grief, I found a lady with a light in her eyes teaching me in a class called "Fascinating Womanhood." I asked her all the right questions and from her heard the gospel for the first time at age forty-one, having been in church all my life.

When I accepted Jesus as Lord and Savior by my bed that night I slept like a baby and awoke with an aura about me that allowed me to float from one place to another with no effort, no confusion, and no pain. I was tempted to think that the change was due to my own efforts. This lasted a day and half, and when it faded I knew I had tasted heaven (Song of Sol. 1:2–4)!

Words leapt out from the Bible and italicized parts from the *Book of Common Prayer*. I often went to morning prayer and communion. Within six months I had experienced a Cursillo weekend (a three-day retreat of prayer and study) and that only intensified the feelings I felt for my First Love. I did not perceive the darkness or shadows that had once seemed to cloud my life because I flung myself into the works of the kingdom. I also sought after the deeper walk in the fullness of the Spirit, and in 1973, after hearing Dennis Bennett, I asked for and received my prayer language alone in my kitchen (Song of Sol. 1:6).

I took in five years of Bible Study Fellowship (BSF) starting in 1974 and worked many Cursillo teams of good works, becoming a team rector (the ultimate) in 1979. I was president of our women of the church for two years. I also studied counseling through lay ministry training during this time.

In 1980 I visited Israel and knew I was a pilgrim wandering home and that I would return. I couldn't sleep at the Sea of Galilee, so I prayed most of the night at my window for everyone I knew. I was looking through the window remembering the Golan Mountains, and I sensed that God was indeed "leaping over the mountains, bounding over the hills" (Song of Sol. 2:8–9). However, as I now reflect back, I did not yet understand the call.

I had remarried five years after becoming a widow, and this marriage was troubled, for John held a hidden struggle. During the next five years I sensed a real pulling back of the Lord. It was probably me pulling back in my codependency to John's addictions, but I felt it was Him abandoning me. I went through much agony these years as I confronted the addictions with the support of some of the clergy—and some rejected me because they did not understand the nature of addiction or the power of denial (Songs of Sol. 2:15; 5:7).

At that same time there was the scarlet thread of divine life that touched me and healed me—an inner healing when I forgave my father (in absentia) for my perception that he didn't love me. In that instant I received instant healing of forty years of allergies. (I didn't ask for this!) Two years later I was able to present Jesus to my dad before he died (Song of Sol. 4:16.)

I was learning the way of the Cross. Along with the inner healing, I was able to step out of denial that I had been too fearful or insecure to see. I lived alone, even suffering the temporary rejection of my own children. I continued from 1984 to 1985 to take classes, usually in the counseling field.

I reunited with John after a four-month separation and remained for fifteen months. Then the final blow came, along with more confrontation by the Book—Matthew 18. This time the watchmen wounded me, and I came bleeding, with a lacerated heart, to Antioch Christian Fellowship, where I have been ever since separating from my friends and the church that was not feeding me. Antioch speaks the Word and walks in faith. I had been wounded again, yet I was tested like Abraham with Isaac to make a sacrifice of obedience (Song of Sol. 5:7; Gen. 22). I know that I am learning the path of suffering and affliction, the servant leadership that is the Sermon on the Mount to those of us who hunger and thirst after righteousness.

I had to contend with more "foxes" as I struggled with my identity and discerning whose I am, yielding to the One (Song of Sol. 2:15). I began to discover that I was worthy. I learned in my heart the twin call of loving God with all my heart, soul, mind, and strength and loving others as myself. In a class I discovered the joy of the Father as Abba. I finally noticed fruit being born out of brokenness (Song of Sol. 4:10–12).

I learned more about my call and why the Galilee had so touched me as I read *Exodus II* by Steve Lightle. I went to a ten-week school of ministry founded by Gerald Derstine at Christian retreat/Strawberry Lake in Minnesota. I continued classes at Antioch.

I began long journeys in my silver chariot (my car) interceding for the redeeming of the land. I went with friends to Washington, D.C., to pray for revival and a return to our godly roots. I call these my Caleb Journeys. I took mission trips to Mexico twice and to Hong Kong to deliver Bibles and an encouraging word.

From 1986 to 1990, through the court battle for the termination of my troubled marriage to

John, the Lord reassured me that the battle was His and that I would come forth as gold (Song of Sol. 2:10–12; 5:11–15! I was beginning to discover the character and loveliness of God as He beckoned me to "Come away."

In 1990 I found that all my persecutors had vanished, and the court trial was over. I discovered in Hong Kong through a couple of difficult border crossings with an intimidator that I am not to give my power away—He gave it to me, and He wants me to wield it. I learned that I was not only a warrior but an army within myself, an intercessor (Song of Sol. 6:10)! I knew beyond a shadow of doubt that "it is God who avenges me and…lift[s] me up above those who rise up against me; [He]…delivered me from the violent man" (Ps. 18:46–48).

Nonetheless, through the year-long struggle in 1990 to sell my home, the feelings of abandonment and rejection returned, along with a sense of being set on the shelf (Song of Sol. 5:6). At one point I cried out, and my pastor saw it as the deeper work of the Cross. At the same time were the opportunities to witness at mission classes and in fellowships.

Finally I experienced release, in several ways. It first came in a word from Pastor Alan that I was being released into my ministry that year. Then, when the court battle was over, I moved from my house into an apartment on Jordan Avenue. It was as though I was finally, like

Caleb, crossing over into the Promised Land as God beckoned, "In three days you will cross the Jordan to go take possession of the land that the LORD your God is giving you to possess" (Josh. 1:11). I went to Russia and Lithuania on September 12 for the next step in the aiding of the release of the Jews, which meant coming into His call for me.

In 1991, as I continued to travel the world doing mission work, I sensed God was making me rise up "awesome as an army with banners" (Song of Sol. 6:10). The more I saw of this Earth He spoke into existence, and the more I became acquainted with its people, the clearer it became that God's creation is like a garden of goodness and justice, and there I heard His voice of love beckoning again for me to "Come away" (Song of Sol. 8:13–14).

Meeting Bob in 1995 was the culmination of all of these experiences. I will forever be thankful to the Lord for the path He orchestrated to prepare me so that I could continue serving Him alongside of such an incredible man of God. Our years together brought novel lessons for me on my relationship with Christ, as I approached Him not just as an individual but with another member of His body so close beside me.

I trust that I have entered into Canaan land, but I never suspected that I would uncover the path I have taken—already written thousands of years ago in Song

of Songs! *Thank You, God, for a wonderful experience!*
Through all of these experiences I learned that I am not
alone in what I have suffered, and I have learned the joy
of knowing my Lord more intimately.

About the Author

BARBARA MELIN WALKER received her ministry degree and license for missionary evangelism in 1993 from Antioch Christian Training School, Int'l (ACTS) in Minneapolis, MN. She is a 1987 School of Ministry graduate from Christian Retreat in northern Minnesota. She also earned a B.A. degree from Northwestern University in Evanston, IL in 1953. Barbara taught school in Illinois, Indiana, and Minnesota.

Barbara's current work is teaching Bible studies, sounding the trumpet to believers for the end times, educating, exhorting, and encouraging through spiritual warfare and intercessory prayer. She felt called since 1984 to bless Israel and assist Jews to "make Aliyah" to Israel.

Contact the Author

You may contact the author by writing to:

Barbara Melin Walker
130 Windsor Park Drive, C101
Carol Stream, IL 60188